Bernd Schlösser

The World "Needs" Psychopaths ......

..... They Steer Corporations And States

Or:

The Augean Stables

Many thanks to Mr. Keith Green, London, for his friendly assistance in translating this book.

A German version is available.

About the Author:

Bernd Schlösser was born in 1960 and was raised in Berlin-Spandau.

In 1977 he began training as a banker and worked in this profession until 2013; primarily in the area of financing for entrepreneurs and freelancers.

Since his youth he played for almost 20 years as a drummer and percussionist in various amateur bands.

Furthermore, the natural sciences were and continue to be areas that interest and inspire him.

In the mid-1970s, a multi-part TV documentary on body language * (gestures, facial expressions, etc.) awoke great interest in him.

In 1987 he started his exclusively autodidactic studies on psychology; initially with popular science reading, later with textbooks for students and medics and study-related material.

The basis and starting point has always been the question of why someone does or does not do a particular act, especially in relation to being destructive or negative, causing hurt or killing. This question extends even to necrophilia (in the context of Erich Fromm).

Many conversations and observations emanating from daily life have compounded his thoughts. His conclusions posed more questions and spurred him into the re-reading of corresponding problems.

His day to day work in the bank provided excellent opportunities to study people from all walks of life, be they clients, colleagues, supervisors, managers or senior officials.

Since 2006 he has lived partly - and from 2013 permanently - in the east of Germany and has become acquainted with both the city life of Berlin and the rural life of Mecklenburg-Vorpommern (a state of Germany).

Although "German" is the nationality printed his identity card, Bernd sees himself as an "earth citizen who just happens to live in Germany".

"With heart and soul and with full conviction I am a mixture of Swiss and French," says the author about himself. "Because in terms of patriotism and liberalism Swiss and French people are impressive and far superior to the Germans. Since the end of WW2, national pride and patriotism in Germany has virtually been eliminated, and the same can be said about the "Right to freedom of opinion" (Article 5.1 of the Basic Law), because it is usual for any one trying to give an opinion to be considered 'right wing'."

* A branch of science closely interlinked with psychology, which brings out what's going on inside us. It is almost impossible to lie with the body. Even deliberately suppressed body signals reveal themselves and ultimately unmask the feeling or even a lie to the experienced eye.

From the Content:

Have you always wanted to know ......

- what or better, who triggered wars - from antiquity to the present day - and for what reason humanity never learnt to finally stop these devastating conflicts? "History teaches us that it teaches us nothing." (Old pupils wisdom) If it is true that history is written only by the victors of a war, then we should ask if we should learn anything from history at all.

- why your boss does not grant you a salary increase despite appreciating all of your and your colleagues excellent work?

- why does someone really wants a "career"?

- for what reason does your neighbour harasses you constantly, even though you are appreciated by all others as a sympathetic and pleasant person?

- or, the other way around - why for many years you have felt and have not been able to explain the notion that people are avoiding or rejecting you?

- why do politicians and business leaders worldwide appear to be largely incompetent?

Why should all this be so, and how can you do something about it? Find out in this book.

Here you will find many, if not all the answers to your questions. This book explains in understandable terms why a healthy soul cares about respectful and peaceful relations. It also explains how we cannot find inner peace and why we fight and harass our fellow human beings, both in the small scale at the garden fence and on the highway, and in the large scale through "legal" conflicts using armed forces and bombs.

The triggers are always the same, but it depends on the intensity, that is: the degree of mental disfigurement or disability.

The reason we do not find more satisfaction around the world is primarily due to the mental deformity of our governments and business leaders, who are obsessed by possessions and personal esteem. This is in contrast to "normal" people who actually aspire towards peace, contentment and a state of happiness.

Mental illness or un-fulfilment stems from the perceived lack of material items an individual believes would satisfy them.

That, for example, edible food is destroyed, while in many parts of the world people starve miserably, has mainly financial reasons based on greed and power claims. An ethically meaningful explanation does not exist.

Numerous small and large companies and providers throw their expired or not so fresh (but still edible) goods in the garbage, rather than make them available to charitable and benevolent institutions or their employees.

That ("livestock") animals are tormented, i.e. kept in too limited a space in the case of the so-called "CC-chickens" (concentration-camp-chickens according to the German press) and that fur animals such as mink and sable also suffer, has only monetary reasons; unless that is the operator actually has a penchant for sadism.

I personally am convinced that way, because a mentally healthy person will not want any part of such actions no matter how much money can be gained by it.

The same is true in my view for people who make and or support animal experiments. Almost 100% of these experiments are not interpretable to humans and are therefore superfluous.

That in recent years here and there things have become a little better for these abused creatures is solely due to the various protection organisations, which work tirelessly for their cause.

Politicians or even the Eurocrats only address such matters when there is no other way and they do so for selfish reasons like wanting to win a few more votes. They do not act through conscience; they only act because of lobbying and in order to improve their own standing. Alas, animals have no lobby and cannot promise "personal benefits".

Even then the transition process to better conditions is based on financial consideration and serves to protect the operators and extend the misery of the creatures concerned.

My work in animal shelters has given me the opportunity to look after animals that hailed from "concentration camp" conditions. It is indeed rewarding to see how well their health and demeanour responds with the correct treatment.

An animal kept in poor conditions that looks neglected on the outside will also be suffering on the inside. This will be due to the release of stress hormones, something antibiotics can only partially treat.

We accept this hormone and drug cocktail with our food. "But how it looks in there, nobody cares ....." (from: "The Land of Smiles", operetta by Franz Lehár).

Life has become a throwaway article, both in "livestock" farming and on the job market.

If you are interested in the reasons behind all these abysses you should read on. Read what, or better, who - breaks us all and why it is.

*The greatness and the moral progress of
a nation can be measured by
how they treat their animals.*

Mahatma Gandhi (Indian freedom fighter)

Contents

What this Book Wants

This work is not only intended to pass on experiences, insights, facts and knowledge, to argue factually and to make everyday life easier. It should also entertain, in one way or another instigate thought. Some smiles and several laughs (which sometimes get stuck in the throat) are guaranteed, despite the serious issues covered.

The book should further stimulate reflection and contradiction, trigger approval, pose choices and polarise alternatives. One can agree with the statements or not.

It should shake up, enlighten and encourage discussions. It wants to move and generate movement.

I would like the remarks to disseminate a spirit of optimism, encourage self-determination and allow this ethos to be taken for granted. Currently of course we are unfortunately very far away from this goal.

This book does not have to be illustrated because in one way or another, any particular event happens millions of times a day. The excesses of our worldwide neurosis-controlled leadership "elite" are served daily via daily press and TV news.

If the reader is prepared to think it through, this book can improve the quality of their life.

The content of this work may be for some readers **breaking Taboo; and that should amongst other things also be:**

Taboos prevent rational, encompassing thought and can serve to create lies.

Even in the case of home-made natural disasters, such as the ozone hole and its effects, the mass extinction of animal and plant species, global warming due to CO2 emissions and rainforest depletion - all human-induced problems - the majority do not seriously respond.

Half-hearted decisions caused by mainly financial reasons slow down and complicate important thought and meaningful action.

As a rule, only the strongest survive in nature, but the most psychologically distorted (and those who join them) tend to survive in Humans, which has been and is mistakenly interpreted as strength in the course of human history. This is finally to be recognized, publicly ostracized at all levels and eliminated as quickly as possible.

The book aims to raise awareness of the pathological processes in the "holy halls" of politics and business.

In the well-known bestseller "Whistleblower" by the authors Jan van Helsing and Stefan Erdmann, the dramatic **effects** of the global "leaders" from politics and business are described.

In this book you will learn the **causes** and how it happens that even the most incompetent people are getting pitchforked into "High Society".

The causes should not excuse the actions of these psychopaths, but the book would like to awaken and contribute to the timely recognition of these perpetrators of humanity, so that they cannot get into the economic cycle.

My advice therefore is that politicians and leaders of medium or large businesses or corporations, be subject to regular examination by independent qualified psychologists as a matter of urgency. Any person in high office failing such a process should immediately be removed from that office.

After the "glassy citizen", to whom we owe the control-seeking state leaders and their vassals, now comes the "glassy psychopath".

Here they are made more predictable and you get a good chance to predict their morbid action and plan: What can be expected from the neurotic, what not, what is to be feared of him and what dangers does he pose?

The author regards this work as his personal contribution to the German federal program "To live Democracy !".

***The truth
you do not need to fear
only the people,
who spread the lies.***

(German saying)

Author's note: I enjoy working with sayings, citations, aphorisms and metaphors. These usually hit the nail on its head with a few words, often bring an "aha effect", sometimes a smile and often carry the maturity and wisdom of centuries in itself.

Sources (including citations) are each provided with tracts in the text. Some information was deliberately omitted to protect people. For the friendly support, I expressly thank all of these persons.

Apropos"Augean Stables": The term found its origin in Greek mythology. Herakles (perhaps better known as "Hercules") had, among other things, been given the task of cleaning the huge cowsheds of Augean, which had not been cleared out in years. Colloquially one designates therefore today "Augean Stables" as a "giant pigsty" and thus as a sign of heavily polluted and corrupt conditions.

Introduction

Who is not familiar with the daily news from the media newspapers, radio and television? Wars, arms trafficking, threats, atomic bomb tests, assassinations etc... You can hardly escape them.

Have we not all often asked ourselves in a quiet moment, why in politics and businesses are so many nonsensical or unreasonable decisions are made - partly against the general sense of justice? Conversations with others make us realise we are not alone with such thoughts.

Our horizons are not limited, but of course in some instances we must take the context of our conversations "with a pinch of salt". Alcohol especially can loosen the tongue but muddle the mind!

"Soberly considered" decisions made "under the influence" usually have no logical basis, although the gut feeling can remain.

Mind you, the term "have no **logical** basis" is for those who are not psycho-**logically** initiated. We want to change that now!

With everything,

- that can not be explained by common sense (rationality),
- remains implausible considering all objective facts and/or
- arguments sound far-fetched,

there are usually two things behind it:

a) selfish, monetary interests, and this in conjunction
b) with decisions of psychopathic persons.

Is mankind conditioned to constantly combat peers, animals, plants and the environment, with the most brutal of methods? Humans deliberately research and pursue the most intense and perfidious ways to kill and destroy as efficiently as possible.

The conquest of new habitats cannot be the sole basis for these hostilities, and nor can intentional or planned destruction. It is just that personal decisions made by (in)competent key personnel often leave collateral damage in their wake.

Of course there are answers to these questions ..... and solutions!

The remarks in this book give the answers from a completely different angle.

Let us take you into a world inhabited by psychologists and psychiatrists.

According to the author's research, the professionals have been reluctant to comment on this topic, and so far no work has been published.

Historically it has been seen as a subject to avoid, as any mention may court controversy.

This is not surprising, because psychologists follow a code of honour (EFPA = European Federation of Psychologists' Associations), although publications of this kind are by no means defamatory or even forbidden. On the contrary.....

There is also an EFPA Media Policy:

"Psychologists have a responsibility to share their knowledge, insights, and expertise with the public. Media (television, radio, internet, {and print} media) have become important sources of knowledge, opinion and influence. By using the media, psychologists can disseminate their knowledge and strive to make a contribution to the well-being of people. "(Source EFPA Media Policy, Preamble 1.2.)

However, why should one walk on the slippery parquet? Psychology can be uncomfortable.

Democracy as practised in Germany and many other countries has a permanent malfunction.

We do not see the shortcomings because we grow up with them, and are blinded by the constant mistakes. We accept the system as normal, yet inside we feel something must be wrong.

In the last few years one could increasingly hear or read in the media the new phrase that he (or she) found "clear words" on this or that topic.

Mostly this has been from politicians who jabbered conclusions and opinions on a topic of irritation (already logical and already known). Care was always taken to be "politically correct" so as not to tarnish the career.

As a rule, something really important and new was not disclosed, yet well-known phrases and platitudes were laboured.

However, the reader will find **really clear and unambiguous words in this little book; that's a promise!**

It should be noted at this point that the author is **not** a "graduated head" in the sense of university education and has **no** academic qualification in the fields of psychology/ psychiatry.

Inventory

To begin with, note the following: In contrast to say mathematics, Psychology, in my opinion, is **not** an exact science. (Psychologists will - of course - have a different view.)

Psychology is an **empirical** science based on long-time conscientious investigations, research and experiences. Yet in the end, despite the best prepared and performed examinations and experiments, the result is never as sure and absolute as 1 plus 1 equals 2, as in mathematics.

To claim psychology was an exact science would in my opinion be irresponsible. No one can read our thoughts with absolute certainty or prove they can. However, it is being worked on and in all kinds of media the very first "successes" are being reported. Thanks to career-oriented brain researchers perhaps thoughts will someday no longer be personal.

Should workable results be found in the not too distant future, you can already bet on what and who will be the first to be seriously interested: The military, the security services and the control-minded state leaders.

A considerable amount of time in the study of psychology is used for statistical surveys, comparisons, correlations and corresponding evaluations. In the end, it cannot be assumed that the result is 100% certain, just more or less true; partly with excellent hit rates.

An experienced psychoanalyst could be compared to a clever criminal who uses a subtle approach (i.e. in conversations) to try to find the best way to get away with a crime. The psychoanalyst does this to liberate or at least alleviate a patient's mental suffering.

„Qui bono?"

A saying from Latin with the meaningful translation: To "Who is this of benefit/advantage?" It raises quite simply the question of the motive: "Why does he do this and that?" We know this from the criminals and the many nightly crime films.

The question of the motif will be encountered again and again in the course of the explanations that follow.

Therefore, the symbol "🔔" for the "motif bell".

(The term is borrowed from the field of photography and means humorously-ironic in that the camera for some rather untalented users, should be installed with a bell that alerts the user to suitable images.)

We question: What motives guide a person and how does he try to reach his desired goal?

His behaviour tells us what happens within a person. But what is normal, what is "crazy" or "insane" or maybe better: eye-catching?

A neurosis (more details on page 21) can be recognised by the behaviour of a person. In order to for this to be recognised, one has to know what is normal or innate for that particular person, and what is socially unacceptable in their daily life. **The difference and the principle are very important!**

If we all paint our faces blue every morning and walk around the whole day, this would be normal and socially acceptable, but would not be normal in the sense of "innate".

In order to give a further vivid and deeper comparison, I would like to make a little digression here:

Shortly after completing my training as a banker in the early eighties, I attended a seminar in the context of internal training with the topic "Detecting counterfeit money".

The seminar leader, an employee of the state central bank, had brought some counterfeit bank notes (called „flowers" in Germany). These ranged in quality from bad to marvellous.

The instructor used a sentance that I thought was simple, ingenious and very informative. He said "to recognise counterfeit money reliably, you have to know what the real money looks like and what features it has."

If "common sense," exists, then this is it.

In order to recognise abnormal psychological manifestations, I must first know what is normal (or innate) for the individual concerned.

Everyone is the Victim of their own Education

What is a neurosis?

A neurosis, or mental or neurotic disorder, is a persistent behavioural disorder that the person in question is aware of (as opposed to psychosis) but can be severely burdensome. General literature tells us that no organic causes have been identified. Further explanations follow in the chapter "About Players, Gamblers and Ill Heads".

Neuroses/mental disorders are contagious, although not in a classical medical way such as in bacterial or viral transmission. Rather, it takes place through educational imprinting.

Even animals can become neurotic by being educated by mentally disabled people. To "sharpen" a dog so that it attacks humans or other animals (which do not correspond to its loot schematic) has nothing to do with education, but rather with an intentional misrepresentation. The fears of humans are transmitted to the animal (one can also say: copied).

Where the "noble" goal is to have your own home guarded, the animal becomes both a tool and the victim of the owner's inner fears and constraints. The "inner worlds" induced the "outer world" it could be said. The neurotic person bends (or adjusts) external conditions to mitigate inner fears.

Babies and very young children are particularly susceptible to this kind of imprinting, as they have yet to develop enough life knowledge to enable defensive or critical questioning.

In the first months of life education is basically a dressage act that can be loving or hostile. The child is completely dependent on the well-being or woe of the persons caring for it. Loss of love, neglect, contempt, etc. (mental maltreatment) can cause devastating psychological damage, and this can happen in the complete absence of any physical abuse.

Although such mental wounds or scars are not visible at first glance, if left untreated can persist for a lifetime and effect, or even dramatically effect the individual concerned.

For example, if such mental abuse was completely clear to public officials in the youth welfare offices, many abused children would not remain with the parents or legal guardians in question. Far better to remove mentally abused children from their abusers, and place them with loving and supportive foster parents.

Bureaucracy, time, staff shortages and the fear of taking responsible action are among the reasons this often does not happen.

Although the legal situation in Germany is clear (see § 1631,2 BGB* = German Civil Code), the methods of education in the local children's rooms (and worldwide as well) will not change and we continue to have empathically supercooled and selfish "leaders" in the respective offices who terrorize their "subordinates" with their infantile frustration.

* § 1631.2 BGB: Children have a right to nonviolent education. Physical punishment, mental injury and other degrading measures are inadmissible.

Obviously, here in the parents' house has been acted wrong, otherwise our "superiors" would not have become as they are and would not act accordingly.

If there is something that could be called a Neu"roses"-greenhouse, then the very early age of every child is it.

An example of this is the previously common practice (although unfortunately it still happens today) of letting the baby scream without response. Even today the "that strengthens the lungs!" view can sometimes still be heard.

A child of this age does not cry to purposely annoy or bully his parents, but does so because it feels underserved. Hunger, thirst, loneliness or pain are the usual reasons. If you are not prepared to properly look after a baby or child, you should not bring one into the world.

Let us put ourselves in the position of the baby, who has no option other than shouting. The baby cannot get up and take care of him or herself. When the infant finally succumbs to exhaustion or learns that his or her screams are being ignored, the noise stops, but the first profound, emotional wound is inflicted.

Another irresponsible nonsense is: "A boy does not cry!" Or "A boy does not play with dolls!" Why should a boy not play with dolls and not prepare for his later role as father?

Boys can look after a doll as lovingly as girls (without becoming a "sissy" or gay); and girls like to play with small cars if you let them. Maybe the little daughter would like to become a car mechanic in later life.

A child in such a family has to live according to the motto "take it or leave it". Beyond that it cannot look "outside the box" as children may do in other families:

"Am I being treated well or bad here?" the child will not know. Are beatings and being shouted at a normal part of my upbringing and education (which is by no means normal)? Does love express itself even though I am shouted at, beaten and insulted? "

The little guy has blinkers on and cannot look left or right to make comparisons.
Only with the child starts to compare his or her circumstances in the kindergarten and school with peers, can an opinion begin to be formed.

By this time it is often too late to change very much, and the child develops with the seed of dissatisifaction growing within, and ultimately passes this onto their own children.

It is just as easy to pass on a loving education, as it is to pass on an education full of fear, threat and neglect.

This is called passive/active reversal: What I passively experienced in my education and had to endure, I now actively pass onto my children, because it would not be learned otherwise. It is a germ that is passed on from generation to generation.

Behaviour, whether positive or negative is also passed onto others in the immediate environment. These may be neighbours, colleagues or other people casually encountered in daily life.

Even experiences that occur in adulthood can lead to feelings of inferiority. It is often said "children can be cruel", and indeed the teasing they sometimes inflict regarding someone's outward appearance can be very hurtful to the soul.

A slightly oversized nose, a harelip, lisp, hobbling through uneven legs or dwarfism seduce children to use nasty words. Also, obesity is commonly used among both children and adults to tease others. If repeated often enough, this too can leave a mental mark.

One psychological principle is: "What has been learned can also be unlearned." This is one of many approaches to treatment undertaken by therapists and, among other things, it seeks to re-educate patients in an attempt to prevent further damaging thoughts or behaviours.

"The smile that you send out returns to you ....." is the wording of a well-known Indian wisdom.

The negative variation of this saying is a "I-hurt-me-permanently-self-tragedy", as it is well known that every action induces a reaction, and that hurting another person always leads to consequence. This consequence may be immediate and active, or passive, where it sticks in the mind and works sub-consciously.

Therefore it is not only that a smile comes back, but - to say it in a sloppy way - even the kicking of someone else up the buttocks!

We often learn through fear (in the vernacular anxiety, see page 55), as we do not want to disadvantage ourselves. Such disadvantages my be the withdrawal of love ("If you do this or that, Mama does not love you any more"), being threatened, shouted at or physically hit.

Such actions often cause tears and physical, but especially emotional pain as well as defiance ("I do what I want"). By way of self-recompense the injured soul rebels, but in so doing injures itself further and does not heal.

For that reason, therapy can be upsetting and often results in the shedding of tears.

However, education does not only take place in the home, at school, in training or in the barracks; in fact it never ends. That is why we are so "receptive" to these fears, if later threatened again. The loss of a job or failure to perform some other task can trigger the distress.

Insurance companies like to work by these means (they say, "rattle the coffin lid.") And politicians like to frighten us with tales of horror that will come to pass if we do not vote for them.

The fact is: **Fear rules the world....**

....and is almost always "distributed" by neurotic people. The so-called authority figures (parents, educators, teachers, supervisors) are then actually "authoritarians" with a correspondingly negative character. Real authorities, however, have completely different values; see in the chapter "The Healthy Soul".

Psychologically healthy people do not "work" this way. The aggressive authority derives its apparent power from the fear of the "subordinates" they teach.

The really timid, however, is the authoritarian counterpart. **Power basically works according to the principle of greater fear.**

We all know or use the sentence: "Be well behaved." Most of the time, threats are promised, or a reward offered to buy the desired behaviour.

If you always meet the expectations of everyone else, you are said to be good or honest.

In order to send assertive children successfully into a world full of neurotics, we should tell them from the beginning: "Always be naughty!"

In adult life, this is called "civil disobedience" (<u>always in the sense of "humanistic opposition" to comprehend and help the entire population</u>), and when the masses join together it can move mountains. There would be no wars, for example, if everyone refused to fight even if called upon by the king.

Acting against authority can be very stressful, especially during childhood and puberty, and when acting against parental wishes.

However, the provocations of a child must be countered consistently.

"Provoking" means nothing other than "I'm looking for a limit!" and "how far can I go?" It is a kind of unconscious request to discover the limit. This limit must be set peacefully, even if it involves nervous tension.

It could be said that the constant provocateur never learnt to respect others during childhood, because no limits were set. Such people will later become big children with dangerous weapons. A representative example is - in my opinion - the North Korean dictator Kim Jong-un.

Another element that children work with is called "defiance", which can involve yelling, biting, kicking and other completely unacceptable behaviour. The child wants to maintain a status and not lose face.

The older the "child", the more ignominious this condition is, and in southern cultures much more than in our country, is considered disgraceful and dishonorable. So-called "honour killings" show where this can lead in extreme cases.

"Defiance" can, as already described above, be openly vented or hidden, where resentment or grief is lodged in the mind.

Hidden defiance is all the more dangerous, because it is never clear when a violent outburst may occur.

Usually the affected person will show somatic symptoms that are not connected with the cause. Now the "big kids" are playing with laws, grenades and ultimately competences that we ourselves, lightheartedly, but subconsciously also follow. The really bad thing is that they are often comfortable because of the suffering of others (i.e. the arms trade).

The competent work of so called expert groups funded by government imposed taxes, can be destroyed by defiance. "I still do what I want" is a common attitude.

That is why the person with the power often imposes his or her will. Not to do so could ruin an aspirational person's career, or be seen as wasting taxpayers money.

Unfortunately, expert groups, working circles and the like, have only advisory functions and no decision-making authority and can be misused as an alibi function.
Back to civil disobedience, which is fundamentally positive so long as it is used to neutralise, or even eliminate neurotic features.

Historic examples of civil disobedience are:

a) Mahatma Gandhi's fight for independence against British colonial rule in India, which came to an end in 1947. This was achieved as part of the independence movement with non-violent resistance, civil disobedience and hunger strikes.

b) The Monday demonstrations in the former German Democratic Republic starting in September 1989. The "Peaceful Revolution" led to the end of the Socialist Unionist Party dictatorship and the fall of the Berlin-Wall.

In such respect, the motto about today's conditions that says

*"Better a government
you can laugh at,
than a government
you have to fear. "*

is undoubtedly correct.

How to Imagine a Soul

The Danish physicist Niels Bohr (1885 - 1962) reported that he developed the atomic model based on a dream. For a long time he had tried in vain to fathom the structure of the atom, but eventually found it in his sleep. We still recognise this same representation of atomic structure today.

It was much later that I learned of Mr. Bohr's strange, but by no means unique experience (there are other similar cases known). I realised that I once had such a dream too, but with a completely different theme.

For years, I wondered what the (spiritual) soul might look like or how it could be pictorially or vividly imagined (the subconscious works in pictures).

Some time ago this dream made me realise how the soul might look, how it works and how it affects our way of life.

My theory is that every one of us carries an inner vessel (soul) with us through our life. This vessel could be a wooden box, a crystal vase or whatever else you could imagine and want to keep with you. This lifelong companion wants to be filled, and this is best done with kindness, maturity, wisdom and life experience.

Anyone who has not learned this via a loving and attentive education will confuse "we live" with "we consume". This is a frequently practiced maxim supported by ubiquitous advertising and nonsensical slogans.

Years ago I read "Advertising is always just as smart as the target audience it's aimed at". It is fact that if the same word-for-word phrases are repeated often enough, brainwashing occurs and the message quickly becomes imprinted.

Just one example that confirmed my impressions. Recently, there were "Fitness buns" being sold at a large shop. Do these buns make me better at sport, make me fitter or slim my tummy if I eat them?

Concentrated bullshit, or simply the targeted anchoring in the brain of garbage-based mottos devised by the advertising strategists.

It is best to avoid products advertised in a demotivational way. Such action is sure to get the marketing brains working.

Inner emptiness and "life values" are replaced by matter that no human really needs.

Many seek a "career" to attain these material things. It is believed the road to success (and the heart of an attractive life companion) is paved with as many credit cards as possible, with a villa on the outskirts and a sparkling sports car ...... or better two.

A medal or a director's title is the goal, and not having either underpins the feelings of inferiority and provides a dubious impetus. More details later!

Claiming power, pursuing a career, wanting to possess as well as excessive consumption are all expressions and

compensation of fears, inner emptiness and insecurity as well as emotional numbing of the same.

But nature can not be deceived here either:
After all, people become increasingly dissatisfied over the course of their lives. This is rarely admitted by anyone, but often expressed in depression due to the craving of material objects. Yet it is only because they cling to the material they become dissatisfied. A vicious circle, founded in childhood and enforced by teachers and other authority figures.

Ultimately, the sparkling, powerful Daimler or BMW (it can also be a Ferrari) is just a nicely painted - but dead - piece of metal and the villa is a polygon composed of simple stone and Carrara marble.

Some people excessively do body-building (there's nothing wrong with moderate exercise!) to show off their muscles (and improve their confidence).

A well-functioning economy and consumer society "needs" obviously sick consumer souls and their psychopathic whippers. The consumer is often guilty by himself of it all because he always demands and expects a "better" way of life, mostly in terms of consumption options.

Example: Meat has to be on the table every day, and this as cheaply as possible and without regard to losses.

Another one: It does not fit into the self-conception of the growth and perfection society that stock prices can also fall. (Who would have thought that?!)

There is great whining everywhere when stock indices fall or a real estate bubble bursts. Then **the** catastrophe is proclaimed and hyped up by the media.

But I say: You ain't seen nothing yet!

Years of hefty profits have been privatized (and are always "forgotten"); Losses are socialized (example: "banking crisis"). This is where lobbyism works exellent and politicians play this protagonist for certain advantages (eg. party donations, advantages in the private purchase of high-priced luxury items) into the hands.

Equally self-evident is the annual family vacation trip (better two or even three) and as far away as possible. Also a popular kind of socially accepted coping with frustration via consumption. Obviously, it has never occurred to anybody seriously that global tourism is not just one of the biggest dirt producer and air polluter (if you think only about the CO2 emissions of buses, cars, ships, airplanes).

In addition, sensitive natural paradises and ecosystems are being withdrawn from the environment, and animals and plants are being deprived of their habitat in order to earn only some million Euros/ Dollars etc..

Ultimately, we owe the plastic littering of the oceans many times to the shipping industry, which prefers to dump its ecologically non-degradable garbage into the ocean rather than have it disposed of in the next port for cash.

Who among us is thinking about that when he books his long-awaited luxury cruise ?! To whom is it really important what the planet Earth looks like, if the globetrotter has passed away in 50 years anyway?!

Not only the globe is victim of litter pollution. As early as the 1950s, we began to cover other celestial bodies (Moon, Mars, etc.) with our scrap in the form of probes, satellites, and measuring instruments. Flanked by irresponsible nuclear tests of various nations in East and West.

The Earth orbit and other celestial bodies of our solar system has mostly been littered for prestige reasons ("race to the moon" in the 1960s, USA and Russia), in each case **wrapped in the mantle of research and science.**

Military upgrading is nothing more than the muscle-wracking of mentally ill politicians with a tendency to persecution complexes, driven and supported by an unscrupulous and greedy weapons lobby.

As the neighbouring countries only wish to live in peace, who is going to attack? Only a neurotic state leader would encourage the citizens of their country towards acts of war, by inventing things and staging provocations.

Many times more money is spent on the arms industry than on projects to combat hunger or protect nature. What is more important, more weapons or a healthy home planet?

Let's go on: Yet others train intensively in the martial arts. ☖ Is their motive to protect themselves, to do sports and keep fit, or to sooth inner fears to become mentally stronger?

Nobody will admit to the latter, rather they express physical, more "noble" motives.

Professional and extreme athletes train for a gold medal or the Ironman and in the long term ruin their health. Many of them resort to doping medication to deceive others, and ultimately, themselves. "The end justifies the means" or victory at any cost.

A particularly interesting group is firearm users, who camouflage their passion with all sorts of noble claims. With a firearm, the mentally weak feel strong, their feelings being bolstered by the gun (similar to the luxury car or a penis extension).

People with this kind of mental affliction like to be seen in photographs alongside weapons, tanks and prototype bombs. A current example in my opinion is the dictator of North Korea. The current relaxed attitude towards protest there should arouse attention and be viewed with deep suspicion.

There are several ways to legally have custody of a firearm. Examples include sports-shooters, hunters, security personnel and police officers.

Much depends on how the user views the weapon, and on his or her attitude toward others.

As a rule, a user with integrity will not, or does not want to talk about the weapon, or consider it the ultimate in their profession. Questions about it are usually answered evasively or not at all (similar to a responsible pharmacist who does not babble on about his knowledge regarding toxins).

On the other hand, the inward wimp is enthusiastic and usually glorifies in the possession of a weapon. Such people will often make remarks such as "don't come too close to me", and is looking for a reason and an opportunity to use the weapon.

The gun narrative and the relevant lobby in the USA speak a clear language, as after a few hundred years the "Wild West", a traditional collective neurosis, is still on stage. Having a firearm means freedom and adventure, even if that entails losing your own child!

How many more shooting rampages, such as those that happen in schools, will it take to bring the responsible (or better irresponsible) law makers to their senses? Rather than ban guns, they make them available to seven years olds!

Yet this is not surprising because self-insight requires self-reflection, self-reflection requires common sense and common sense is based on a healthy soul.

Just as a psychopathic boss abuses his personal skills and seeks to legally bully his employees, the neurotic gun fool (at least in the imagination) is looking for an opportunity to take a shot.

Let's continue the topic:

Still others have tattoos or piercings all over their bodies, enlarge their already considerable bust size, have Botox injections or alter their appearance in an array of other ways.

The main thing is, to make he or she stand out and grab the limelight.

The rainbow press satisfies two collective neuroses in one fell swoop:

a) The need for recognition by some of the wealthy aristocracy and by those in the television and film industry who „cannot get enough of themselves", crave to stand in front of cameras and revel in awards and self-adulation, and

b) those living in jealousy and curiosity who seem to have no life of their own and pity themselves.

Hard words, yes. But the truth tastes the more bitter the farther you have gone from it.

For what reason is there really no Oscar, Emmy, Bambi or similar for say the "Precision Engineer of the Year"?

Advertising is everywhere and the market is full of products that propose to spice up the ailing little soul. The "Shopping Frenzy" is a proven outgrowth of emotional emptiness and can lead to disaster, especially of the financial kind.

Luxury items are always in demand, even in bad economic

times.

The cosmetics market and the slimming delusion with its various pills and powders are a "billion-dollar" empire that plays on the minds of those with self doubt.

In this context, I remember a sentence from Billy Wilder's feature film comedy "One, Two, Three" from 1961: "Capitalism is like a dead herring in the moonlight. It shines, but it stinks! "(Role: Horst Buchholz, a famous German actor).

Capitalism is fine so long as it does not only benefit a few people or harm the environment.

I recall an experience I witnessed at a car dealership some time ago, that I found rather sad.

A customer wanted to install a "sound generator" to make his engine seem more powerful than it was.

I thought I had mis-understood, but the dealer later gave me an explanation.

Sound developers are booming in the car industry, and they exist solely to give the illusion of quality and power the buyer cannot in reality afford. In other words such devices exist to make the neighbours jealous! Car fun in "Imitated Edition"!

If that's not enough, others go to image consultants to learn how to look more appealing to others. Politicians, the image conscious and those who want a "career to the top" are the main users.

A scam, because you lead other people behind a light show you do not represent (and ultimately you do not represent to yourself), whereas if you had the necessary self-reflection, you could represent the people honestly. The image consultation is almost a mask-and costume rental, nothing else....

It is therefore **never** about the content, but only about staging and the exterior; so hot air only ....

Most people are constantly
busy becoming something;
the least, to be something.

Our inner poverty will remain if our little soul vessel is filled with substitute matter.

If you are rich inside, you do not need this frippery.

Conclusion:

It's hard work
to be so superficial ......

The Healthy Soul

The mentally healthy person sees himself as an individualist. Peer pressure plays no role to him. He is self-confident in his way and "does his thing", if necessary alone (as the famous German singer and entertainer Udo Lindenberg, whom I personally consider a strong individualist, would most likely say).

These people cannot be harnessed to primitive ambitions or feel life as a river with all its comings and goings. They usually do not have a problem letting go, and consider "mistakes" more akin to life experiences.

This testifies to inner freedom and true greatness. They are looking happy to the next day and know very well in advance that they will cope satisfactorily with whatever it brings. They may be authorities, but they are not authoritarian.

It would be better if these inwardly free authorities were the leaders, rather than those who just want to be leaders. 🔔!

The problem: Internally free people do not stand for election because they do not feel the need to dominate others. Psychologically healthy people feel like one of the whole of mankind and feel no need to go in any other direction.

The vernacular says with a wink that each of us has his "tic" or "birdy". That is certainly true, but not meant at this point.

These feelings can build up and cause an immense amount of suffering for the person concerned over time. This stress is often directed toward the immediate environment, and the recipient may be the life partner, the children, colleagues or anyone encountered during daily life.

Frustrated or neurotic people get to a point where they "explode", and although they may then feel better for a short while, the bad mood returns soon enough. Subsequent rages result in shorter and shorter periods of relief. It is rather like drug therapy where the dose must sometimes be gradually increased as the body gets used to the medication.

There are many rungs on the "job ladder", and some people will do anything to climb it, even if it involves flirting with crime.

The fact that the recipient is almost always not the cause of the frustration does not matter to the psychologically ill, and neither does the personal bad feelings that follow.

Mentally sick people quickly feel instinctively uncomfortable in the vicinity of mental health, because they realise that they cannot do anything to impress.

These "subjects" are often treated by using crude methods. One can say, they speak different languages, and what man does not understand, man fights.

The psychologically healthy and biophilic (= life affirming, biophilia: love of life and all living) people can be recognised by the following characteristics or behaviours:

He (She)
- respects all skin colors, nationalities and religions.
- has no problem apologising sincerely for his mistakes.
- uses natural resources such as food and drinking water sparingly and wisely.
- is a pacifist with a natural need for freedom.
- would like to be socially "present" and recognised and respected.
- has a natural, friendly and relaxed charisma.
- has a liberal world of thought and worldview.
- does not think about dominating other people; but does not want to be dominated either, and defends himself mostly in a passive way.
- cannot be pushed into drawers or made to follow tight regulations.
- is (for the most part) free of fears and inner constraints.
- never enjoys the misery of others.
- never tortures animals, not even professionally or as part of a job (animal transports, chick shredding, laboratory tests, etc.). He finds this deeply unethical and rejects it categorically.
- does not throw truckloads of plastic waste into water or arrange it (not even as a job and for money).
- will not join or form any political parties or secret societies.
- has a strong sense of activity.
- is spontaneous and open minded toward new things.
- is respectful and considerate toward fellow human beings and their environment.
- is rather inconspicuous and quiet in nature, but confident and not shy.
- reacts openly to constructive criticism and listens with interest.
- can say "no" without feeling guilty.

- likes to share, even if there is little (selflessness); but will not be exploited.
- is sociable, but also gets on well alone.
- can realistically assess themselves and their own abilities.
- is as a mentally healthy person inertly strong but does not need to use this strength.
- feels close to nature and everything that lives.
- is not resentful and is ready to forgive.
- provides a clear path without being hurtful.
- has no problem praising and appreciating others.
- looks to the future with calm confidence and reacts flexibly to it (adaptable).
- respects the health of others and their own.
- does not require from others what he or she is unable to give.
- does not care about titles or awards.
- cannot be overburdened or concerned with matters that are hopeless from the outset.
- tends to be humble, does not care for social climbing and does not crave financial wealth (these people have inner wealth).
- to put it in modern terms, does not circulate PC viruses and does not "hack".
- will not destroy edible food, even if it is part of a job such as retail, catering; see also above under "never tortures animals ...."
- is cooperative (in positive matters) and willful, generally finding a solution to every problem (while the neurotic seeks and usually finds a problem for every solution).
- does not build massive walls, fences, fortifications or cause this.

These features (viewed in a more or less emotionally balanced state) appear with different intensities, from more to less to not at all. There are as many variants as there are people.

The list above is not in order of value or exhaustive, but gives a good understanding of the "Healthy Soul".

Those characteristics do not describe "super-humans", just those born that way, which actually is not an ideal state. This already gives us a certain sense of how sick our everyday life appears.

It is important to mention that so-called "healthy egoism" is intrinsically normal. This includes the impulse to survive and involves the aggression instinct (controversial to psychologists), which aims to fight and kill if necessary (hunting, protecting the group), to feed and ultimately to survive. In this respect, there is a certain contradiction.

However, one can hurt such a stable and positive person internally, when the hurt is intentional and targeted. A broad front that offers itself here, amply used (mostly by superiors or the spouse who "has the pants on") is always camouflaged with "noble" but selfish motives to maintain their own status.

The attacked person will not act out his or her frustration on another person or object, but target the origin which often is his or her counterpart.

Unfortunately, children are born who are mentally and or physically disabled. From a sick soul from birth in this sense, nothing has yet been learnt. There is however, research that deals with the extent to which prenatal experiences can lead to such mental deformation, such as violence inflicted on the mother during pregnancy, and so-called birth trauma.

It is said that the soul of all human beings, whether born in "civilization" or among people of the Amazon, is fundamentally the same on the day of birth.

It is subsequently altered according to education, which could be affectionate and considerate (liberal), or rigid and unloving. The first year of life and in particular the first few months, have the biggest influence.

In any case, mentally strong people, as described by the features above, are not endlessly resilient. In each case, the adequacy of an action or reaction must be judged against the prevailing circumstances.

For example, the death of a close relative will invoke a much greater response than more run of the mill issues. This is normal.

What profession is best suited to those described above? A mundane 9 till 5 job in a large bureaucratic organisation, with many narrow minded regulations, would be frustrating to say the least. Certainly they could be successful, but many would eventually opt out.

Better would be a career in the artistic or creative fields, or to establish their own independent business. This may not give them the biggest financial income, but it does offer much better job satisfaction.

A mentally healthy person does not need to follow a formal religion, as their inner feelings compensate. This is not to say they may not wish to mark a special occasion, such as the passing of a friend or a beloved pet, with the burning of a candle, but it will be a personal decision.

I regard myself as a "pantheist", meaning "God is in all", or "God is at one with the cosmos and nature". There is no personified God here, but there is nature and creation in all you can see, hear, smell, taste and touch. One should perceive with all senses.

This gives a good state of mind, yet so far as I know, there is no institutional church set up with such ideals. An old English proverb says "Seeing is believing", and in pantheism no one is dependent on faith because everyone can see nature and creation.

Within pantheism there is nothing and no one to impose their will, faith or wish for material gain upon me. As a follower of pantheism I am completely free of mind, and do not have to pay taxes to a faith.

-Nobody sends me, as with the "Jehovah's Witnesses", to ring the bell of other people and convert them to my way of thinking.

-Nobody compels and educates me to fight or regard other faiths as "infidels", as is the case with some realms of Islam. After all, we are all just human beings. To call a war "holy" today is ridiculous, and warrants admission to a psychiatric clinic.

-Nobody makes me feel guilty because of the actions of my forebears, who for example, may have been involved in the Holocaust. I cannot change history, and money will never compensate for suffering that has already been inflicted.

Overused words such as "Antisemitism" and "sedition" do not mean very much. They are however a proven way to keep liberal and forward-thinking attitudes low or nipped in the bud, although in my opinion they lack any factual basis.

Incidentally, the term "anti-Semitism," as used by "state organs" and the press, is factually wrong and serves only to intimidate citizens. An authentic definition is found in the corresponding educational works that provide neutral and above all, **factual** information about the term.

Every being, including man, happens to be born in some area or land. Nobody chooses this.

For this reason I will not blame or imply an "original sin" toward German politicians as has been done for decades. It is a shame that there is no paragraph against "national dumbing down" in the law books.

Who preaches this in Germany and professes to be public and quite natural, is undoubtedly always on the "right side", which is conducive to any kind of (political) career.

Every human being should consider themselves citizens of the earth, rather than being assigned to any arbitrarily prescribed "tribe" or nation.

Intolerance and greed, serious psychological weaknesses, have long led to animosity and violence, especially between religious groups. Unfortunately this will continue in the future, as our leaders are unable (or unwilling) to keep their beliefs personal.

All religious wars since antiquity have been caused by the intolerance and greed of a few soul-suffering rulers. Ultimately, all wars are based on emotionally deformed leaders, whose "noble" reasons mask their own inner discontent. Fear of dissenters and who do not understand (or want to understand) drive these aggressions.

The inner thoughts of humans often transgress to outer actions. We'll talk more about that later.

Many years ago in a church magazine, I read a definition of religiosity that touched me deeply. Unfortunately, I cannot reproduce the exact wording, but the message was something like:

"A religious man takes as little as possible from another life." Something that pertains to animals, plants and everything in between.

Those who lead people into war and inflict death on all other forms of life via bombs and other weapons cannot be religious and therefore cannot be mentally healthy.

Exactly the same applies to terrorists of all shades; I regard dictators as belonging to them, but with arbitrarily legalised means. Error in the head = (T)error

Ditto, those who deal with weapons (governments included) and those who exploit and harass others as part of their professional lives.

Those who demand unconditional obedience,
will have unfair intentions.

And:

Who lives in inner peace with himself,
is not tempted
to declare war on others.

About Players, Gamblers and Ill Heads
(The Glassy Psychopath)

In the daily application of the worldwide psychological knowledge and research results available humanity is still acting like in the Middle Ages.

After all, the German legislature has become much more sensitive to the behavior of bullying (§ 223 STGB = German Penal Code sets in here) and stalking (§ 328 STGB).

However, the clear evidence is usually a problem, especially since many matters of facts are not displayed. Partly they are downplayed and/or the victims abstain from shame on an ad. Unfortunately, emotional wounds such as outer ones are not visible or hard to detect.

Bullying and stalking has - indeed - a criminal offense as a physical injury, eg. beating. So give your boss quite an ad in view, if you feel emotionally threatened or even injured, and inform his supervisor of this.

On the political level and in commercial enterprises, the "fist law of the prairie" still prevails. I have often experienced how destructive management deals with bank employees, although one can and should presume some education, including empathic nature.

We are more or less consciously in contact with **physical hygiene** at a young age. Industry and advertising pour us with soaps, fragrances, aggressive detergents, cleaning and care products, which should be better reserved for the chemist.

As white as possible (better still pure) should be the laundry, or optimally: Sterile as in the operating room (but detrimental to our immune system, which, in the case of infection, it has no more practise to defend itself. This is, among other things, the basis many allergies).

A billion dollar business ..... and extremely harmful for the environment!

Remember, everything we dump in the sewers will one day come back to us as drinking water. It's just a cycle. It is proven that not everything can be completely filtered out by our water treatment plants (eg. estrogens, microplastic particles). Enjoy your drink....

Vaccinations, screening, surgery, etc. complete the picture of our physical care.

For the **intellectual hygiene** usually provides the respective government of a country. Not without self-interest, because often one wants to take away from ordinary people thinking; whether he wants it or not.

Government circles and their institutions ensure that, f. e. certain books can not be read, and documentation and reports disappear in the drawer before they become published. Press and media become synchronized and manipulated.

A smack of paternalism is difficult to suppress.

Unfortunately, there is still a shortage of **psychic hygiene**. More about this - especially for daily exposure and remedy - reveals the book in the following chapters.

People with a neurotic disorder often experience considerable mood swings and are often seen as insecure, anxious and inhibited. The anxious often live a mental lie, but hold their views in a stoic way.

A neurotic tends to first notice the **bad** in people, whereas a healthy person will, most likely, first notice the **good**.

This will usually result in a sense of inferiority and a need to compensate through appearance or intimidating behaviour. One could think of this as an "inner pair of scales".

On the left hand scale are the learned misleading motives. Psychology likes to use vivid examples such as prisms or lenses, and these distort the real facts.

This leads, through the wrong misinterpretation of the real situation, to a completely wrong or inadequate response, or indeed no response at all.

To balance the scales and make the neurosis tolerable for the patient, the balancing weights, or compensations, must be placed on the right-hand scale.

These conspicuous behaviours and symptoms, of which the patient is often unaware, are only reflected consistently in response to the environment.

Another, rather "classic" - albeit very simple, but accurate definition of this mental disorder is: "Neurotics suffer from life."

One could also say that they vie their environment and surroundings as an opponent. It is no wonder then that they often send out a certain amount of destructive energy and a signal of resistance. Almost always they are on the defence against a fictitious threat.

This sense of "one is against me" or "one does not appreciate me" is mostly due to the unconscious experiences or traumas of childhood. The former early childhood feeling of not being loved, being abandoned and being unable to defend oneself is relived again and again and projected onto others as if they were the cause. Basic trust is reduced or missing, because at the beginning someone did something wrong.

It is interesting that a person with neurotic disorder does not want to be thought of as rude as he or she deals with their fellow human beings and the immediate environment. They naturally give themselves more rights, consider themselves something special and want to be touched with velvet gloves.

At this point, internal conflicts have created an important and treacherous discrepancy that delicately interferes with social living. "He or she likes to beat but hates being beaten."

Anyone who does not feel secure in a **rationally** dangerous situation (for example, being in a lion's cage together with that "lovely cat"), will try to escape as quickly as possible. This is called **fear,** and to psychologists and physicians it is clearly distinct from **anxiety**.

Anxiety comes from within, can occur for no rational or recognisable reason and as a rule lasts longer than fear.

The diffuse anxiety in the neurotic disorder causes the affected person to understandably seek ways to alleviate the condition. In some instances this may involve the avoidance of certain situations, such as surgery.

In the long term, the path of life is influenced because decisions are made time and time again. In each case these decisions are coloured by the neurosis, which makes the condition worse. The inner thoughts of this person are inseparably connected with his or her decisions!

Careers with high aspirations are often begun so as to compensate for the feelings of inferiority, and to satisfy the need for self-appreciation and social acceptance. Such decisions are commonly supported by people who are equally emotionally burdened (Mentor supports Protegé).

The American actor and comedian Danny Kaye (1911 - 1987) knew the following about having a "career":

"There are two ways to make a career: either you are really doing something, or you are claiming to be doing something. I recommend the first method, because the competition is not that big here. "

The career path could be described as a kind of escape, because he or she does not feel well among his or her peers. Working in a world with other neurotics who share the same mind set is a much easier place for him or her to live. Here, too, one can say: "People of the same kind stick together" and "one speaks the same language".

As a boss, all others have to "dance to my tune", so his or her fears are pushed to the back of their mind, possibly balanced and better controlled. There is no need to enter into a discussion where his or her shortcomings may be highlighted. The "boss" simply instructs, and the employee is not expected to object.

If so, this person may be branded as one or all of the following; unruly, incorrigible or non-team-minded. This is of course more likely to apply to an inflexible or intolerant boss.

Especially in the professional world and in hierarchical structures, it is not respect that is given to "superiors", but pure fear. This is often confused.

It becomes problematic when the employee dares, because of inner strength and a healthy mind finds counter-arguments and serves them in a friendly manner. Unfortunately, by virtue of hierarchy, the "awkward" employee will be the loser (although morally the winner) and the neurotic boss will feel better affirmed in their position of ill aspiration and continue to manage in a poor way.

Now is the time to live out the everyday whims and to pester employees according to their supervisor's mood. Counter-arguments are quickly interpreted as insubordination and punished administratively. The human resources department functions in the same way, and will (almost) always reinforce the decisions of the superior, because the internal lenses of the personnel manager are also blinkered. The personnel manager can hardly fall to support "his" leader, because he may have hired this mentally deformed person himself.

Just as a dog procreates a dog, inability procreates the inability.

In addition, neurotic leaders are completely inadequate and unable to give objective employee appraisals and credentials.

Professional advancement promises privileges, such as a private office (demarcation to the "common people"), possibly a company car, salary increases, bonus payments and in larger companies, even a title.

Ergo: You can become all in life if the sense of inferiority is strong enough. **This is why** you very rarely meet nice and understanding (read: mentally healthy) people in managerial positions.

The air pumps are usually found in the first row - the nice and understanding people are usually found in the lower ranks and are usually the ones

- who understand,
- have knowledge,
- accomplish something real,
- survey the chaos

- work very well,
- do not thresh phrases
- and often cover the crap their superiors fabricate.

In summary, one can say:

***The one can be recognised by their deeds,
the others by their fuss.***

Many will recognise their boss in the description given above. If this is so, I suggest you place a copy of this book inconspicuously on their desk, or give it on behalf of the team, nicely packed for his or her birthday.

The above-mentioned suffering is often inflicted (acted out) upon the immediate environment, and family and work colleagues often take the brunt. In such cases the lack of obvious reaction successfully mitigates the ill persons deeds.

This may continue for a long time until

a) someone successfully fights against it or
b) the person in question stumbles over their arrogance and shortcomings (perhaps through incompetence), or
c) the suffering grows until it can no longer be controlled without therapeutic intervention.

I am aware of a case in which a whole department (about 12 employees) had opposed the airs and graces of their leader.

Result: The team was replaced whilst leader remained at his old post. These are "true" leadership qualities that one can be "proud of", and which go through a whole company and destroy it from inside. Competition becomes superfluous. By the way, that company does not exist anymore because of wrong investments and overconfidence on the part of the board.

"Careerists" often conspicuously neglect and or dominate their families just as they dominate their enterprise or "subordinates". They are cool, calculating and have little empathy.

These are regretful figures who can only articulate themselves through power (the oppression of others) and possessions.

Not infrequently they join various clubs and groups, to conform and climb the career ladder through personal contact and false friendships. The associated board work etc. is usually imposed on others.

One might suspect that for the description of a psychologically conspicuous person one only needs to turn the features mentioned in the previous chapter into the opposite. This may be partly true, but it would be too simplistic, because the whole thing is much more far-reaching, multi-layered and absolutely rewarding to be showcased.

Neurotic people are usually identified by the following behaviours (although not completely, as I do not want to stir up prejudice or cause unfair judgement). Often, several features interact with each other in different intensities.

Some of the characteristics can be sugarcoated, and these are then identified as "leadership qualities" that are highly welcomed by those who are neurotic themselves. If the transmitter and the receiver are adjusted to the same frequency, anything is possible! Even extreme criminal acts.

These people are true energy devourers and "soul ticks" who suck the force from everyone's psyche.

Here too, the adequacy of the reactions to the given situation is to be observed:

He (She)
- looks phony, stiff and wooden in the movements (especially good to see by dancing).
- is likely to respond in an extremely jealous and possessive way,
- can appear very vain and fish for compliments,
- puts great value to exuberance,
- struggles to praise and appreciate others (this they consider to be a weakness).
- appears cocky in speech and body language; have blatancy (which is otherwise known as a "busybody").
- only understands their own problems and ailments.
- is hardly or not at all capable of accepting criticism (the vernacular also says: thin-skinned); then rises voice quickly and gets loud.
- has little or no self-reflection.*

* Self-reflection: The ability to critically question the own situation by yourself, your actions, and your effect on others.

- overestimates frequently,

- is conspicuous and overly ambitious. Is often busy and pretends to show an "important" face.
- likes to praise themselves a lot and is convinced it is justified. Has permanent self-congratulation and makes remarks like, "I could have done a lot better than you did", or "I knew it before.....",
- hardly misses an opportunity to belittle others or their achievements or ignores such altogether,
- talks badly out of the ear-shot of others (the "rumour mill"),
- often appears dominant, brash and overbearing,
- is overtly gleeful,
- gives themselves more rights than he or she allows others. ("If two do the identical thing, it's not the same thing."),
- always wants to be in control (this includes the data collecting mania of public authorities). They are aptly referred to as "varicose veins",
- has a tendency to imperiousness and acts in a dictatorial way,
- withholds important information (which especially at work can cause blatant damage),
- likes to humiliate and torture others and does not feel guilty about doing so (sadistic tendency),
- spies and uses negative things to enhance his or herself,
- reviles other people's achievements and or talks them down or ridicules them,
- likes to use others for personal goals but is unwilling to repay,
- demands from others as a matter of course what he or she is not able to do or willing to give.
- uses old rope teams (i.e. from study periods), in order to "climb the greasy pole",

- is suspicious of new things ("No Experiments"), but requires this from his fellow man and is then very curious about the result.
- is not marked by modesty and tends to be less economical with resources, especially with foreign funds such as taxpayers' money.
- "loves" all people where it benefits them (so-called soapiness, vulgar: "brown-nosing").
- glorifies the supervisor, yet ridicules the "subordinates" who are "infantry",
- hunched up, step down (in the vernacular: "cyclist").
- finds honorary title (acad. degrees, director, etc.) highly desirable and fascinating,
- needs a lot of space in speeches and loves "big" gestures, i.e. far-reaching stereotypical arm work (well observable in political speeches).
- is prone to breaking promises,
- likes to use other people's help but drops them later,
- likes to hide behind rigid rules (insecurity before creative and free thinking),
- is easily impressed by wealth and "great deeds" (i.e. splendid buildings),
- is mentally rigid and has a closed mind with regard dissenters who may have reasonable arguments,
- is jealous of the success and or the possession of others,
- has a tendency to bitterness,
- tends to be uncooperative,
- finds it very difficult to apologise or say "sorry",
- finds it difficult to be reasonable,
- has a strong tendency to lie. If he or she is caught, the "Salami tactic" is often used: Only admit, what can currently be proven.

- is looking for "whipping boy" or someone else to blame,
- likes to judge and condemn,
- prefers mind decisions. Decisions that come from the "gut" are virtually nonexistent. Everything must be reasonable, rational and put into rules and paragraphs.
- has a tendency to be disrespectful in tone, but only toward "subordinates",
- likes to cling to fixed specifications and forms, and finds creative
suggestions diffuse and frightening,
- tends to be arrogant and haughty (arrogance is described as the distance caused by insecurity and possibly fear),
- tends to monopolise conversations or discussions, to interrupt others or to let them speak,
- confuses goodness with weakness,
- serves his superior submissive and overzealous with anticipatory obedience.
- likes nepotism.
- is a supporter/advocate of lobbying.
- is not averse to corruption if it serves the career.
- tries to make everything perfectionistic and so heavily burdened his fellow human beings.
- honors and strives for privileges such as VIP status at XY, boasts with thousands of flight miles per year and all variants of "noble" credit card editions, etc.
- considers attractive partners as property and trophy and has a tendency to isolate them caused by jealousy.
- defines himself (almost) exclusively about property and power.
- begrudges others nothing, but everything to himself.
- threatens fast with the lawyer.

- threatens fast with physical violence and does so without hesitation.
- feels empathy and sensitivity as weakness and is extremely ignorant and resistant to learning in this regard.
- uses "gaslighting" (a perfidious manipulation technique that ultimately makes the victim doubt his or her mind and can cause serious psychological damage). Please refer to the relevant specialist literature.
- reads this book to find out how he/she can manipulate and exploit others even better.

And:

High-aged men still father children (so-called "own grandson producers").

These features occur with different intensities, sometimes more, sometimes less and sometimes not even at all. There are as many variants as there are people. Of course the list above can also be supplemented and does not follow a specific order.

In serious cases symptoms include:

- Striving for power against all odds and rules.
- Using the instrument of indoctrination (no contradiction allowed and no discussion).
- The loss of grip: "Everyone must share my opinion," or "everyone must do as I say."
- A tendency toward criminal and unscrupulous actions,
- Feelings of omnipotent fantasies and megalomania (" the guilty are always the others, because I am faultless.")
- Equality with God….

At the level of heads of state, this is recognisable as follows:

-The medium or long-term melting of democratic structures and values,
-finding "guilty" persons and falsifying reasons to remove unpleasant people from office (fake coup attempts etc.),
-The dismissal of those with an opinion different to the leader,
-The proclamation of emergency conditions to justify greater leadership and military capabilities,
-Appointing relatives and friends to government related positions (nepotism),
-The numerically far reaching dismissal of civil servants and the like,
-The threat to instigate further measures to deprive selected groups of their rights,
-The censorship of press, radio and television,
-The organisation of groups of thugs under the guise of the military to intimidate the population,
-Brutal persecution to end protest by the masses.

Furthermore, the actions of a mentally ill person are characterised by cowardice. Such a person does not want to know the consequences of their actions, and choose to hide behind a barrage of regulations, socially accepted excuses and legal jargon.

Examples:

- The "simple" employee or office manager who hides behind the service regulations, and has no idea about initiative, creativity or improvement strategy.

- The drunken and notorious racer who chooses to hide behind their alcoholism rather than face up to the deaths caused by their driving.

- The Chancellor who hides behind the decision of his or her committee or waits for an EU directive. This is a crude blurring of personal responsibility and an anonymisation. Read more on page 90.

Yet it would be so easy for politicians to absolve their responsibiltiy were they to implement a people's referendum. More on this topic later.

In the above mentioned scenarios, the focus is mainly on the natures and traits of leaders and presidents of dictatorial regimes who possess fascist tendencies and profess (pseudo) democracy.

Although Fascism as a term is difficult to satisfactorily and tangibly define, it is essentially characterised by:

- Anti-liberal behaviour, where dissenters and minorities are defamed, interned, killed, removed from office or receive public ridicule. There may also be silencing of the press, intimidation and manipulation of election results.

- Anti-social behaviour such as the removal of children from their parents, or the persecution of a particular clan.

- Nationalist thinking (ie. "America First") and the selfish belief that "we are everything and you are nothing at all". In my opinion this shows a lack of foresight, immense irresponsibility and is of psychopathic significance. The Berlin Wall was built on flawed foundations, as are the discussions regarding the proposed US-Mexico Wall.

- Leadership principle worshiped as a cult, with agitation, sedation and incitement of the masses against dissenters.

With this knowledge, you should have an excellent overview of the full extent of human interaction. Normal is only **that** we treat each other with rudeness and irreverence in everyday life. However, in the native sense is this **by no means normal**.

The reader can now decide for themselves whether for example, Donald Trump got lucky in the political game of lucky dip, or not!

....or Mr. Erdogan is a democrat as you can read in the schoolbook.

It may be that someone reading this book recognises some of the traits listed above in themselves. This would be, according to the well-known antique saying "Know thyself", which is a highly positive experience.

"Self-knowledge is the first step to recovery" and therefore the first step in a more positive future for all parties concerned. It takes a lot of courage to scrutinise and question oneself critically.

Self-test for self-reflection:
Listen carefully to yourself what you say to others in which manner and then ask yourself whether you want to be addressed that way.

Often strong contradictions, anxiety and possibly aggression will emerge in response to issues or lies that are identified or revealed. The human being is likely to disclaim, deny, combat, disparage, ridicule or invalidate the contents shown here. In no way will they constructively deal with, accept as a possibility, approve or attempt to implement any of the contents.

This is especially true of people who have become comfortable with the existing system, and are doing "well" in it (i.e. officials and lobbyists), or those who have issued themselves an excuse or "fainting pass" ("There is nothing I can do anyway.").

Finally, strength and firmness are feigned on the outside, but barely or not at all exist inside. However, this will not work because the person is betrayed via body language via stereotypical movements (i.e. leg-paddles, playing with the pen, curling hair strands, etc.) and by the cramping of muscles.

Close observation is not necessary. Suppressing the (micro-) motor skills, the facial expression (poker face) or consciously practicing omission will usually reveal other observable signals.

The feeling is always stronger than the will and finds its way out!

There is no authenticity or credibility in those who try to deceive. Credibility only comes with expressions of straight thinking, straight talking and the taking of actions in good faith.

"False" behaviour (the pretence of self-confidence) attracts the empathetic person. Real self-esteem does not stand out. It is pure inner strength as well as energy and goodness, and comes from being "over-the-things" others are not.

Arrogance is self-confidence
of the inferiority complex.
(Edmond Rostand, French poet and lawyer

In which occupations will we find people who more or less practice "false behaviour"?

Primarily this is in large institutions and public authorities which provide "protection" behind rules and regulations. In my experience these people do not understand the reasons behind the rules, they just enforce them. If questioned they just say "that is how it is" or "dodge the bullet".

Petty business and the care of beneficiaries are thick pillars of bureaucracy, whereas expediency and flexibility are more fragile. The system does however create and maintain jobs in state and private sector administration.

These people love to impose a superior attitude and delight in jobs where they can force others to fill out lengthy forms and then wait in draughty corridors. They do so and hide behind a system of bureaucracy for protection. Examples may be found within the judiciary and those who hold executive posts. Judges, prosecutors, prison staff, police, financial service staff, administrative officials and employees at all levels of public service, may also relish such roles.

Such people of course also exist within in the private sector although here the ice is considerably thinner, because companies usually rely on their customers. Unlike within the public sector, these customers come voluntarily and can switch to another provider.

It means: Where there is no competition, I can show and make others feel that I am the boss.

Public servants often forget that the individual citizen is actually their customer, and it is they who pay their salary via their taxes.

Although this **may or may not be the case, there are distinct tendencies.**

By chance I once saw stuck on the PC monitor of a Berlin official at the registration office, a note that said "The official channel is a way for "too lazy to think"- employees,". Wow, there was a very brave man, or perhaps he was frustrated or wanted to end to his career.

But there is something about the motto, "if you are creative and have an eye for usefulness, you can get the work done in half the time".

The free economy also has similar jobs to offer, such as hiring managers, employees in HR departments and chief secretaries who often delight in playing a "lofty" role.

Likewise, the various religions also offer career opportunities with very strict hierarchies. Anyone who is afraid of their own freedom of choice and likes to serve submissively will fit in well.

Another way to falsely fulfil one's self esteem to to bully salespeople, who cannot defend themselves because they must always be friendly, especially in difficult situations. These same people will complain sooner or later anyway. Yes, the customer is king, but only as long as their behaviour befits a king.

My tip to all managers of abused employees is to throw the upstart customer out and loose the revenue, no matter how high it is. No customer is worth your co-worker being humiliated! In the long term it will be harder to replace a reliable and already trained employee. Stand behind your staff, say it and show them!

Some "character traits" are socially recognised, welcomed, praised and rewarded. Compulsion to control, the enforcement of rules and exaggerated ambition are desired by employers who present such traits as "good examples" to their wider workforce.

I would like to mention the symmetry compulsion here as it is of interest. Those afflicted feel compelled to align everything as symmetrically as possible. Such examples may involve the meticulous arranging of cutlery, desk utensils and tools. What may at first seem amusing can develop into a serious nervous affliction. In the UK it is known as an Obsessive Compulsive Disorder (OCD).

These behaviours are not only a sign of mental illness, but they also make coexistence and work relations hellish to others, including their own children. It is damaging to companies due to lost production, and costs the health insurance sector billions. This trend has increased over recent decades, as often reported in the daily press and news reports.

It is undoubtedly even "better" and "more advantageous" for disabled souls to help shape legislation at source to help them pursue a political career.

Unfortunately our media seem to support the view that the well off are better supported in the law courts than the general public. It has been reported for centuries that "the little ones are hanged, and the big ones are allowed to walk."

This is a further incentive for psychologically deformed people to persue a great career, as then they can allow themselves to walk unpunished from wrongdoing or unscrupulous practice.

For example, no judge will jail a Chancellor, "only" because he has committed perjury in court or obstructed or veiled the investigation of a serious crime (including coercive detention).

I give you my word of honour on that!

Can you imagine a jailed Federal Chancellor?

Me, yes!

Conclusion of this chapter:

***His deeds
betray
the psychopath.***

Case Studies

In order to loosen up the theoretical explanations mentioned above and to make the practice clearer, in this chapter I would like to share with you four short and hopefully entertaining case studies from my professional practice or personal peer contact.

For the outsider this may be amusing, but for those concerned it may be nerve-racking. In the following only the names of the persons concerned have been changed.

1) The Steinhuber Case: .... leads by bad example.

Mr. Steinhuber is head of a middle bank branch, in his early 50s, is married and has one child.

His reputation precedes him, he has not shown much in the way of initiative, and the HR department would like to move him to a quieter branch. He is not needed in his current post because his staff, mostly aged in their 40's run the bank very well without supervision.

Mr. Steinhuber works away from the bush drums of the shop floor, and prefers to spend his time in his consulting room at the very back. His door is normally closed so he does not have to see the "misery" (quote!) that goes on at the counter zone and in the counselling area.

A desk within sight of the customers does exists, but usually is only occupied by the boss **before** or **after** opening time. As soon as the bank opens, Mr. Steinhuber bolts into the refuge of his consulting room. Perhaps he fears contact?

Sometimes during opening hours, staff have to "disturb" him in order to obtain a permit, and when they do they find the following:

Mr. Steinhuber sitting cosily reclined on a comfortable chair, studying the daily press, the Financial Times or the "Frankfurter Allgemeine Zeitung", with his legs crossed whilst sipping a coffee with milk. His shoulders visibly cramp when the staff member first enters the room.

On other occasions such as when a customer asks to speak with him, there are two possibilities:

a) If Mr. Steinhuber knows the customer to be pleasant, he will sit down and have a nice chat over a coffee. Time passes by and the daily newspaper is put aside for later. The long afternoon is then whiled away in the pretence of studying the stock market or some other issue.

b) If the customer is unknown to Mr. Steinhuber or has something unpleasant to say, Mr. Steinhuber becomes visibly annoyed. Sometimes he will ask the employee to deal with the matter, but if the customer insists on talking to the "boss" the situation deteriorates, especially for the employee. We shall find out why later*.

If the big chief visits, Mr. Steinhuber ensures all the trivial details are attended to (such as making sure brochures are neatly displayed) so as not to risk any awkward questions. Mr.

Steinhuber does not want to "rock the boat" of his comfortable asylum. He represents very well the phrase "do not get noticed".

The brochure stand is of course up to date, the curtains fresh and the trainee well-groomed and friendly. Not because of Mr. Steinhuber, but because the staff themselves are fit and attentive.

Mr. Steinhuber also demands this, but says it is his doing. He says "No experiments!" (as in the 1957 "Adenauer elections"). Any transgression is punished with a bad review at the next employee assessment.

He keeps a small *black book in which all "mishaps", such as which staff ask him to speak with customers are noted. He probably cannot even remember any blatant faux pas made by his staff.

One customer once spoke to me at the store on a sunny morning during opening hours and said, "I saw your boss walking down the Havel River with a camera. Doesn't he have anything to do?"

Well, how do you answer that and remain a loyal and honest employee?! All I could do was to give a tormented smile and an insecure shrug!

Just how Mr. Steinhuber managed to ascend to his senior salary position was a mystery, until we give it some thought.

Could it be his supervisors were equally incompetent?!

Conclusion:

*A well-functioning firm can
endure at least one lazy person.*

2) The Krumm Case: So cramped, that even his hair is stiff.

Together with 20 co-workers, company director Mr. Krumm was head of a corporate customer care department. He had a company car and all the trimmings one could wish for. He was in his late thirties, presumed to be married and always a bit stiff in manner.

He rarely if at all spoke about private matters, and certainly never to his "subordinates". No one even knew therefore if he had a house or a garden.

Occasionally he used words of English vocabulary that made him sound *international* and educated. In so doing however, he sometimes gave something away during conversation.

It was always clear he adored his boss. Whenever he could he would say that Mr. Jensch was a great man! Those two have known each other since school and have often socialised.

"I'll have to talk to Mr. Jensch about it first!" was and is a popular sentence from Mr. Krumm, who will then make sure he cannot be blamed if something goes wrong. Mr. Jensch would then be able to find another scapegoat to blame.

Everything had to be perfect if Mr. Jensch visited the department. Mr. Jensch himself did not seem to appreciate the constant flattery of Mr. Krumm, and this showed in the micro-motor activity of his face. That spoke for him. Yes, yes, the "lick icon" of flattery is chiseled in slime!

It should be noted that Mr. Krumm's position gives him far-reaching powers and privileges. It would be better to have Mr. Jensch in place of Mr. Krumm, and in so doing save the opulent "Krumm salary" and make big cost savings for the company (the black luxury BMW limousine would go for a start).

Mr. Krumm does not like employees to question his authority or make suggestions of their own either.

Sometimes he likes to talk in detail and at length to his employees, and becomes frustrated if they have to excuse themselves to use the toilet. He does not even make allowances if the toilet break is due to a medical condition.

The Krumm monologues were generally boring and led to intellectual absences among those targeted, who often dozed off. Mr. Krumm would then let a ball pen slip out of his hand to bang loudly on the desk. A more respectful tactic would surely have been:

a) to make the speech shorter,
b) to make the lectures more interesting,
c) or to train in speech dynamics in order to better gain attention and reduce monotony.

Better still, it would be preferable not to listen to those who like the sound of their own voices at all.

Mr. Krumm is usually short with his time, issues e-mail type instructions and is mostly unapproachable to other office workers. However, a hyena-like grin suddenly starts to beam with joy over his whole face after a "devious" employee asked Mr. Krumm to explain the different titles and competences required by the firm's directors!

Mr. Krumm's eyes lit up and he began to speak at length. He droned on about the title that he currently (still) has and about the filigree differences between him and the individual whose job he wants. Mr. Krumm sat on Cloud nine and, together with the cloud, he floated out of the room, to the next customer advisor, to repeat it all again.

One day the computer crashed in Mr. Krumm's office and he could not open a very important and much used program.

A program that provides current account balances detailed sales, credits and direct debits. In short, all the important information required to ensure the management and monitoring of the business.

This program also gave Mr. Krumm a degree of control over the credit limits given out by his co-workers, and the reasons behind them.

It would have been easy for Mr. Krumm to call the necessary department in order to rectify the fault, or even to get his very competent secretary to do it for him.

Although Mrs. Sandman was a respectful and unimposing young lady, voices fell silent whenever she entered the customer service office.

However, the call to the department was not made because Mr. Krumm did not consider it important. He thought he had enough staff to perform this "low grade" work without the computer, so the matter remained unresolved for many weeks.

Subsequently, an until then honest account manager, began to make some mistakes, and started approving increasingly higher credit conditions to several long standing companies.

Any banker reading this will instantly be alarmed!

The whole matter ended up in court and cost the company damages of a seven figure sum. The corporate customer advisor concerned lost his job, and I later found out lost any career prospects as well, privately, too.

If Mr. Krumm had got his computer fixed when he should have, the whole matter would never have happened.

Perhaps the mistaken colleague, with a strong warning, could even have kept his job. We do not know what Mr. Jensch said about the incident, but the Krumm career never fully recovered. Not too long later, he unexpectedly grabbed his things and left the company. He said of course this was "completely voluntary". The bush telegraph however, told a different story.   "Anyway ....."

Conclusion:

Pride goes before a fall.

3) The Case of Dr. Müller: Lack of self-reflection

In order to classify a lack of self-reflection as a layman, one should internalise the following event:

Dr. Müller, is a Doctor of Psychology, a customer of a German bank and almost 70 years old:

He wrote to the bank's complaints management because he was not addressed by a bank employee using his doctor's title. It was later learnt from the branch manager, that an apology from the employee and the store manager had not been sufficient.

Certainly it is rude to deliberately omit a title if it is known, but I am convinced this did not happen, or if it did was completely unintentional. Either the employee had no knowledge of the title, or had simply overlooked it on the account records.

That Dr. Müller was very proud of his academic degree, we of course understand, as undoubtedly it is a big achievement. This he never became tired of emphasising time and time again in a subsequent phone call. After all, he had only begun his studies and doctorate after finishing his professional career in the seventh decade of his life.

My first thought was when I heard this was, why is someone still studying psychology at this age? In so doing he probably took away a university place for a young, aspiring, interested person and made the matter worse by going on to do a doctorate.

At **that** age he would not practice any more as no clinic or medical unit would hire a nearly 70-year-old psychologist. He could of course set up his own practice, but as far as I know (and thank God) this was not planned.

During the telephone call, which was to clarify the facts, Dr. Müller was from the beginning very dictatorial, and stated that an apology from the bank branch was by no means sufficient for this "gross offense". He wanted a higher department involved, and for the lady employee concerned to face disciplinary proceedings.

Of course, the complaints management once more apologised but stated "the misstep" of the employee was definitely not intended.

Surely no other subject of study completed at such an advanced age would compel such a response and end up at the Complaints Department.

However, as a psychologist Dr. Müller knows the workings of the mind better than most, and how to manipulate them.

He clearly had an exaggerated need for recognition and narcissism*, together with a lack of self-knowledge.

For me personally (I apologise for this presumptuous "judgment"), I consider Dr. Muller totally unsuited to the position of psychologist, which exists to help others recognise themselves and bring about mental recovery. I hope he really did not intend to practice anymore.

(* **Narcissism** stands for everyday psychology and colloquialism in the broadest sense, for the self-love and self-admiration of a person who considers himself more important and valuable than those judging him It is also defined as exaggerated self-love and egotism.)

Conclusion:

Why do you look at the speck in your brother's eye, but fail to notice the beam in your own eye?

(See the book of books, Matthew 7: 3)

4) The King Case

Mr. King is a bachelor in his mid-40's who does not have children and is always correctly dressed. He is a consultant in the credit department at a headquarters, prepares loan applications from the branches and makes them ready for decision. Within manageable limits he has his own authority for credit approval.

He can be described as choleric-aggressive and visually likes to use the "threatening finger" with his voice raised so as to warn employees about their own decisions. He does not appreciate the thoughts and suggestions of employees, as he considers only he is right. However, he always expects others to to think along. For what, was always a mystery ......

Now and then he makes fun of the emotions of his subordinate colleagues. About a tiny, cute teddy bear on the desk of one such colleague, he asked "as an adult, how can you put such a silly thing on your desk"?

To the credit counsellors of the bank branches and respective bank branch managers (even the very patient), he is like a "red rag to a bull".

Mr. King is known as hyper-meticulous. If you meet him personally, his face will be screwed up almost like a "clenched fist". Hardly anything can satisfy him.

A good mood is a foreign notion to him, and when he laughs, it sounds cramped, false or sardonic. For him, the rest of his colleagues are "all idiots" (citation!).

In general conversation he is condescending, cynical, disdainful, and partially faecal-tinged.

Mr. King has a colleague called Mr. Bartmann, who has the same responsibilities. He is a bitter man and complements Mr. King magnificently in everything he does.

Mr. Bartmann and Mr. King make an excellent team so long as you do not care about business turnover.

In the branches, credit consultants and branch managers exchange internal company information, so it is known that even promising credit inquiries are rejected in advance. One avoids the nerve-wracking discussions with Mr. King around the "Emperor's Beard".

This has earned the two the internal nickname "Loan-Defence-Department".

And: Don't you dare give a loan without collateral, you bad boy! Best obtain new 100-Pound notes in double loan amounts due to inflation!

Whoever acts authoritatively

cannot be an authority.

How do you Deal with Everyday-Neurotics?

In particular, supervisors can, as briefly outlined above, be a real scourge.

We already know that people with neurotic dysfunction are fundamentally insecure, anxious, inhibited and need to defend themselves against fictions issues.

We as visitors (customers, guests, clients, patients) are perceived as a kind of enemy, yet we do not want anything bad for our counterpart. We only want information, a few rolls, a corn plaster, the mower repaired or some other trivial service.

Under no circumstances one should provoke and pour oil into the fire, but these people are very susceptible (some seem just like a spider waiting to pounce), and sensitive. They look for provocative words and phrases so they can respond to their "enemy" in their usual way.

Ergo: Always stay friendly, never respond to insults and do not forget you are dealing with a sick person!

These people get all the more annoyed if you do not communicate in their "language".

A remarkable anecdote from my time at a bank branch follows:

A customer has complained to me about a trainee because he

was (too?) friendly and accommodating. This remained an isolated case through almost 4 decades, as usually, customers complain when they feel treated in an unfriendly way. However, as this customer was known to be problematic, the young man acted correctly. Always stay friendly!

A popular farce of the vernacular advises: "Imagine the people naked."

A certain ridiculousness defuses the situation, at least in **our** heads, if there is anything to defuse. Over the years, I've come up with a slightly different, but similar, method.

I imagine, I am a staff member in a clinic (my virtual environment) for mentally ill patients. As such it is well known that our patients must not be upset or irritated in any way (quasi first commandment, you choose to study this subject in order to deal with the mentally ill).

That's why I say "yes" as often as I can, and I answer "okay" when I'm approached. Logically, these people come to you with requests you cannot or will not meet. It would also be irresponsible to hand over the key to the asylum, so you don't do it.

Of course this is not always feasible, but even a soldier does not need to follow nonsensical commands.

A similar trick of the mind would be to imagine, instead of the above-mentioned clinic, a kindergarten in which one is the head. We are all children and will remain so for a lifetime, not necessarily in a biological sense, but in a mental one. This is especially so within our family setting and for some with the psychological disorder akin to "infantilism" (a keyword).

The purpose of intimidating through arrogance, loud and cocky behaviour, within a large and chic office is always the same: These people are (usually unconsciously) afraid, just as small dogs bark loudly and grab for the heel. They bite out of fear.

If you are looking for a promotion and or a salary increase, you may choose to praise your boss. This is balm for his rushed and "misunderstood" soul, **but it** must be convincing, be served subtly and must not come across as "soft-soap".

Essentially, a career is about saying what others want to hear. You have to believe in nonsense, do you not?!

Bureaucrats of all Countries Unite: The EU....,

.... the extended arm of the BRD or: Bureaucratic Republic of Deutschland (Germany).

It is clear from press reports that in the EU, Germany is repeatedly leading the way and dominating. Sometimes it is patronising towards other states, especially so in tax matters, about which it is best not to joke with Germany.

Other countries, other manners: A conversation with a high-level Spanish embassy employee in Berlin made it clear to me that undeclared work in Spain is also forbidden, but in general not too strictly regarded or punished. And that is for good reasons:

1) The persecution down to the smallest detail, such as raids on tiny construction sites by the German Customs Authority in order to unmask unregistered foreign workers, costs more than it ultimately returns to the state. There is little evidence such actions deter future transgressions either, as is proven by the constant repetitions. The often considerable financial damage caused by the customs authorities, due partly to massive meddling with the day-to-day running of the firms, does not seem to concern the officers. The owner of the company concerned shoulders all of the trouble.

2) Experience has shown that the money from illicit employment in Spain tends to reduce social security benefits. This not only relieves the public coffers and administrative expenses, but also says something about the decency of the Spanish population.

However, the EU and indirectly Germany say this cannot be, and interfere in a world that did not wobble until they became involved.

Whilst the forerunners of the EU (the European Economic Community and the European Community) had the sensible goals of strengthening economic ties, strengthening international trade and promoting economic growth after the Second World War, things changed in 1992. In that year the European Union took over, and soon became a playground for prestige-minded politicians and regulation-maniacs.

The wish was to emulate the political system of the USA with their states. They wanted, like a small child to play with the "big boys".

Indeed, some German politicians are dreaming of a (cit.) "United States of Europe"!

However, a matter that is always gladly misunderstood and repressed, is that the USA has a completely different history.

The United States was founded only a few hundred years ago and grew organically due to large scale immigration over the last few centuries. On the other hand, the countries of the EU had been independent, with their own identities and cultures for millennia.

This was a serious issue from inception, as was the presumption that each "EU" citizen would honour the new way.

The structure and trillion-euro graveyard was from the outset a witless conglomerate of ragtag countries, of monetary incentives and a stage for sick souls to let off steam.

The personal freedom of every state is written in a lower case, and because a state consists of its citizens and not just of its representatives (which is generally forgotten by them), it also restricts the freedom of each individual.

This requires an adjustment until self-abandonment, which has to be displeasing for each native resident.

Who cares how crooked a natural cucumber has to be, or how big an egg?! That should be reserved for the diversity of nature. The market itself regulates all this according to supply and demand (first semester, study of business administration, EU-responsibles can surely go to be a guest auditor and should make full use of it!).

The overly crooked cucumber remains lying (or maybe not) aside, the little egg also (or not). Next week both cucumber and egg will not be offered for sale. So simply works the Market economy, and sustainability!

Everything else is regulated by the DIN authorities (Industry Standards Association) or industrial companies. They are best suited for this, because they have the respective expertise, are close to the market and through necessity, know all the requirements.

However, this is too uncomplicated for regulatory-neurotics who take great exception to normative or numerical procedures. In one of his books, Peter Lauster (a well-known German psychologist and author) called it a "lust for norms".

Individuality is made flat because it is unpredictable and that scares these ill people. As a consequence of this neurosis, millions and billions of people as well as nature and the environment suffer.

An immense part of their identity and individuality has already been taken from the citizens of the associated states by the stealing of their currencies. There is hardly a German alive today (who is old enough to remember), who does not mourn the passing of "his" D-Mark.

Who was asked if he or she wanted the Euro? In really important questions, no referendums are held by the "leadership elite". They know only too well the outcome would most likely get in the way of what they wanted to do.

The Swedes were much smarter as they rejected the introduction of the Euro in a referendum in 2003 (!). The always neutral and for centuries independent Switzerland, one can only be congratulated on their whole policy.

However, Swiss bank secrecy is being undermined, especially through the interventions of the Germans who want to make the Swiss feel guilty.

German politicians, especially embittered finance ministers, forget that money is primarily in the home where it feels safe, and is not the focus of envious neighbors and investigators.

And who tells us that the data CDs of alleged tax evaders purchased by the German government under dubious circumstances did not contain addresses of German and/or European politicians, "high-ranking" officials and important lobbyists? **Who controls the controllers?!**

In the German thought process everything must be fair, predictable and as complicated as possible, no matter what it breaks.

However, the EU has one big advantage for the respective chief politicians of each country. Unpopular and inconvenient decisions, which may cost votes, will be transferred to another level, that is, to the anonymous institution that is the EU.

An additional advantage is that "I" cannot be held responsible for this because the EU has made this decision "anonymously". In this way you always have a diffuse whipping boy as culprit, who is as tangible as a slime eel in the Atlantic.

But, the dirt you put under the carpet is not out of the house yet. The art of "cleaning" is to distribute the dirt in such a way that it is no longer visible.

"Alas", this is a tactic that only works for a certain amount of time. This eventually manifests itself in the blatant dissatisfaction of some states, and results in actual EU-state exits or bankruptcies. The British can only be applauded because of their courageous and certainly rewarding decision to leave the EU.

The exit of each country is an attractive new step into freedom, independence, identity and individuality. All these are the things that hurt and confuse people with neurotic disorders through their lifetimes. That's why equality is the trump card in the EU, as the uncertain future becomes a little more predictable and less frightening for sick souls.

The idea that there will never be 100% certainty is unbearable for these people. It is therefore largely repressed, and becomes a life lie.

The Pound has been retained by the British, so they were spared a change of currency.

The support measures for bankrupt member states are completely irresponsible. Each banker learns in the first semester: "Never throw good money after bad." This means you do not give more credit to an entrepreneur who is (as good as) broke.

You let this company go bankrupt, because nature makes it happen, what rots will decay and produce something new and produce fertiliser. If the EU finally collapses, it would leave a lot of fertiliser. After all it has been stinking for years on all corners and edges.

Only the market regulates what and who survives. Darwin's "Survival of the Fittest" also applies the economy. The strong survive whilst the old and the weak fade and give way. Yet many subsidy projects distort the market and delay bankruptcies. By the way, bankruptcy can be a criminal offence leading to the loss of liberty, but obviously not if you work as a Eurocrat.

The amount of money spent by this deadly body to keep alive energy and vehemence is truly amazing. On the other hand, if you were to dissolve the EU, it would be a confession that all of our "working" politicians had done something wrong. For mentally ill people this is an impossible prospect and thought, although it's not their money that's pumped and dumped there.

If "professional politician" were to be a vocational training, these irresponsible mistakes would not happen. These mistakes are after all obvious to every trained and mentally sound businessman.

Permanent EU "wiggle candidate" Greece, for example, was got into the EU after some back-and-forth by a not even intelligent math-trick during Kohl's Chancellor era in 2001. This revenges itself now sustainable.

The EU:

- a project born of self-love and delusion of power,
- a spiritual-mental cemetery with graves self-made and an inability to act,
- a "Hall of Shame" and nuisance to every citizen,
- an Eldorado for spiritually dead people who want to exercise power and
- for people, full of inner uncertainties and constraints;
- created by failed existences for failed existences .....

Billions of taxpayers' money, earned by millions of hard-working people across Europe is being plundered here. Most ironic of all is that these people are then terrorised by largely meaningless laws and regulations they are forced to fund.

In recent times the EU seems to have made some sensible decisions, such as the recognition that there must be an end to the plastic littering of the oceans and that we must stop exterminating insects.

Unfortunately, the final ban of pesticides and herbicides remains difficult, because too many lobbyists stick with the lucrative status quo. Let us see at what time they finally realise you cannot eat money!

It is a strange thing that always these people who are not able to rule themselves, want to instruct others.

In any case, I view this only as human self-interest. After all, the seas can no longer be exploited for fish, and without insects no fruit or grain can be grown.

In this instance, the insects are only a means to an end, which is to feed the people. If these tiny animals were not part of the food procurement cycle, nobody in public office would care about them at all.

We learn:
Entrusting taxpayers money to a politician
is like Dracula guarding a blood bank!

Why We can do Without Politicians Worldwide ..... and Have to

Who would expect hard, physical work from a physically disabled person? Certainly none of us would. From such a request, we would turn away indignant.

Which of us would expect a person with learning difficulties to solve complicated mathematical equations correctly? Certainly nobody, as the thought is absurd.

So as a matter of course why do we expect psychologically challenged people to consistently make far-reaching decisions that have momentous consequences in all areas of our lives?

Obviously we all do, and without any deep concerns or regard for the consequences at that. Is it some kind of blindness, or does convenience prevail over self- determination?

Every decision that we and others make is based on respective, very personal psychological traits. This is as inseparable as it is unthinkable to entirely separate our professional and private lives. It is an illusion, as it is as impossible as a blind person becoming an eyewitness!

Herein lies the danger that anyone who co-decides for others, wants to co-decide, so fights hard for that ("🔔" motive?) which best suits his highly personal beliefs, likes, dislikes, affronts, and preferences.

A head of a family can bring happiness to that family with all decisions and actions, or bring absolute catastrophe.

People, consciously and or unconsciously, stamp their own mark on each decision. A parliament can and will serve as a brake, but in the long run can never completely prevent the will of the last decision-maker. The Turkish leadership has been a vivid example for years, as step by step it moves toward a totalitarian system, or get there by some other means.

It is already 5 minutes **after** twelve, and we urgently need to switch to an improved worldwide democratic system, or in some places to introduce a democracy in the first place.

No politician will be enthusiastic about it (**they do not have to be**) and they will use every argument, be it senseless or based on predicted fear to fight back. You have to listen carefully and ask yourself what is the substance of what has just been said. 99.9% phrases are threshed, just as in advertising.

He or she see their perks swimming away and fears for their dear benefice. It is all about the selfish motives of the "representatives of the people", and not about that which makes the people of the nation feel better. Anyone who has gone through a nerve-racking career progression does so for themselves, not for others.

A similar problem, claimed to be democratic, are people's referendums. Many intentional hurdles stand in the way of implementing a referendum in Germany.

In my opinion there is no plausible reason for this, but we can talk about it. In order to plausibly represent the will of the people, the hurdles must be set much lower.

Referendums, one might say, are equivalent to the curtailment of competencies, as they limit the absolute scope of action a politician or panel can take. They cannot do what they want.

Referenda are setting boundaries to self-glorification, megalomania and "landlord's arbitrariness".

But if a person has nothing to fear and the work is done well and in good conscience (if you have one), why not let the people have their say or make a decision? If change leads to more satisfaction, so much the better.

In my opinion, the prevention of democratic decisions derived from people's referendums are anti-democratic, and only successful in involving as few people as possible in decision making.

The opinion of the people is demanded again at the run up to the next election, but to be exact, only on the day of the election. The voter stands at the centre and therefore in the way. The next day he has to disappear again into the mire of insignificance. The voter is an uncomfortable appendage of democracy.

Kurt Tucholsky (a famous German author) is credited with the following quote: "If elections change anything, they would be banned."

The opportunity to initiate a referendum or petition for a referendum on our Austrian and Swiss neighbours, largely the same in language and culture, is much easier to handle and understand. (See respective Federal Statistical Offices as well as Federal Constitutions Switzerland, Austria and German Basic Law).

A comparison in round numbers, as of 2016/2017:

Switzerland: 5.3 million eligible voters; 8.3 million inhabitants; 2.0 million without Swiss citizenship

> a) Popular initiative includes the right of (even!) one
>   to obtain the desired constitutional amendment;
>   100000 voters in 18 months
> b) Referendum : 55,000 Voters in 100 days

Austria: 6.4 million eligible voters (already aged 16!);
         8.8 million inhabitants

a) The referendum initiators must obtain an application for authorisation to hold a referendum. This application requires that nationally, at least 1 per thousand of citizens identified at the last census, must submit a so-called valid "statement of support" to officials at certain offices; currently well over 8,000 votes.

b) After that, the actual referendum takes place, according to which, at least 100,000 signatures of eligible citizens are to be submitted by the initiators within one week (registration week).

Germany: 61.5 million eligible voters; 82.8 million inhabitants

The referendum procedure in Germany is extremely complicated and confusing. **Who would have thought that?!**

On topics to which the citizen should be invited and encouraged to participate, to shape, to contribute their own ideas, high hurdles are imposed. It seems to be a "prevention tactic", which ultimately serves no purpose.

This is basically a three-stage process.

Thus, there are widely varying regulations within the country i.e. in Hessen and Saarland rules have been so strict and restrictive since the founding of the Federal Republic that no referendum has ever been held there, until now. In other states, the rules are less strict and partly used.

The guidelines on how many voting citizens have to cast their vote within which time varies from one federal state to another. So far there has been no agreement (or wish to agree) on a common denominator.

In addition, certain topics are fundamentally excluded (i.e. the free-democratic basic order and the constitutional order). Depending on the federal state, there are other topics that are excluded from a referendum as well, such as public taxes, the budget and pensions.

Here the citizen has no voice, although they financed everything via their taxes and various other payments, and woe to everybody who does not pay his taxes properly!

But note the much cited sentence in Germany: "All state power comes from the people." (Article 20.2 German Basic Law). For this reason, we presumably do **not** choose a Federal President in a direct election.

Obviously, German citizens are not trusted on this matter. The argument that this is so in the Basic Law (Article 54 et seq.) is not taken seriously. Laws are there for the people; not the other way around. One can change (almost) anything, if the will is there.

The issue of referendums in Germany is so complex that it goes go far beyond the scope of even this book. If you are interested I recommend you select and read more detailed texts yourself. You should take a lot of time, be well rested and be in the mood. (See the numerous federal and provincial laws, constitutions, etc.). I believe politicians in Germany have little desire to allow a referendum, and will do all they can to deter or prevent one.

There appears to be no liberality or closeness to the citizens. Some German politicians even claim that a matter, which could include a referendum, would be too complicated for the average citizen to understand. (It would therefore be an important task for German politicians to prepare these topics accordingly and to explain them to the people in a comprehensible way.)

There is a feeling the citizens must be protected from themselves. Who does not suspect paternalism is behind this, and the declaration that the citizen is more stupid than he actually is.

If one follows this idea further, one can come to the conclusion that the citizens of Austria and Switzerland would have to be wiser, because in those places (see above), there is a much more liberal right to referenda. Or perhaps the politicians there can better deal with popular opinion and better trust their citizens.

While everyone has to obtain a fishing license to pull a few sprats out of the pond, there is no training for responsible positions such as "member of the board" or politician. Although the banker has at least a bank education, he or she has no state-approved or recognised training for leadership.

Obviously then, anyone can lead without exams, because it cannot be so difficult, and in any case it is easier than bringing the said fish ashore.

However, this is a momentous fallacy because on these floors we have, due to their psychologically illiterate and underdeveloped minds, a conglomeration of unsuspecting laymen, stumpers and amateurs!

"Professional" politicians are often lawyers. I once heard this is so because they can best free themselves from the mess they have wrought through verbally contorted legal manoeuvers. Here is the probate "salami tactics" popular stylistic device.

And some are not able or even too lazy to do a doctoral thesis on their own. Some prefer to plagiarise.

There is an urgent need to appreciate one thing: The people at the base usually have honourable motives, want to make positive change and do good. Unfortunately, they are often ruthlessly used and abused as tools of power.

With the local politicians and mayors, even in rural areas, power claim comes into play, and even at this level senses become nebulised by the scrabble for power.

For months, I have been thinking hard about whether I should list the current concrete examples of wrong decisions made by our "leadership elite". However, I decided to do so would be akin to those who throw eggs and tomatoes, so have not.

After a few months, the mistakes are forgotten, because nothing and no one has a memory as bad as the broad public.

And to our (un)happiness politicians worldwide provide us daily and reliably with new embarrassments. They tramp (or trump...?) from one confusion to the next, ensuring it never gets boring and allowing the past to repeat itself constantly in various shades, but with no less damage.

The daily press provides constant news and entertainment about the concentrated incompetence in business and government circles.

Selflessness, altruism and strength is seldom found within these ranks.

Also, who will remember any Kohls, Merkels, Wulffs or Schäubles in 20, 30 or 40 years?! At most, a history teacher will maltreat his bored students with the "yesterday's eternals".

Hardly any of the young people will be seriously interested in engaging with Adenauer's, Strauss' and Stoltenberg's. Who?

Mighty people have virtually never completed or overcome their adolescent childhood, and continue in the same way.

In this regard, **they have to be considered failed existences right from the start. So if you strive energetically and intensively for a responsible job (🔔 motive?), you have already disqualified yourself for it.**

This is because he or she will undoubtedly and always have their own selfish preferences in mind.

Thus, we come to the advanced "noble" motives, which are served to us in a full-bodied way.

Of course the candidates will not tell us that as a rule they only represent their personal well-being as woe, who would choose such a person then?

In one of his satirical sketches from the 1970's, Otto Waalkes, a well-known German comedian, described this clearly and aptly. On the fictitious question: "Where do I stand politically?", he answered, "Main thing, I'll come in well, sit fat (get fat like a grub) in it and must not out again (do nothing)!" Mr. Waalkes has "looked at people's mouth".

Why does he succeed where our executive committees do not? The answer is conceivably simple: He is mentally healthy!

Of course, Mr. Waalkes will never stand for election as Chancellor or Premier, but as a comedian, he would have a good chance of becoming president in the USA.

The Americans have been practicing for this ever since the election of Mr. Trump!

The polished version of the candidate voters get to see, is one of a wholehearted, selfless individual, committed to representing and increasing the good of the people.

This is the usual wording of the general oath of office. It is a wonder that the Bible does not burn many a hole in the hands of those taking the oath (in a religious sense).

In the course of my private studies, my opinions concerning world order turned upside down in my head, but became perfectly clear:

The gutter is not along the street with its shady characters. It found its way into palaces, government offices and executive floors worldwide, several thousand years ago. This is not only so in terms of luxury living, but also so in terms of an inner attitude toward others.

The blanket of civilization that envelops man is extremely thin. A very fine scratch brings the primate in us back to the surface. So does the impression which intensified in the course of my autodidactic studies and continues.

After all, we are all just primates who dress more or less chic and sell each other things that nobody really needs; a ridiculous picture.

From what we can see and hear from TV reports and newspaper articles, it seems to me like drunken chimpanzees constantly throwing faeces at each other.

Augean stables, exactly! And as North German people like to say: "The fish stinks first at the head!"

By the way, which chimp will you vote for at the next election?

***People who have learned to
sell themselves well,
usually have nothing to offer.***

(German saying)

What Power Does

"Power" is the name of the stage on which mentally disabled people exercise their neuroses. Power is, figuratively speaking, a crutch to keep a sick soul going. This preferably requires a legal (although it does not have to be) framework in order to let off steam with impunity.

The desire to obtain power is a behavioural disorder. It is based on the principle of being able to impose one's will on as many others as possible, and is driven by their own unsureness.

Therefore, mentally ill people do not belong in parliament or in the executive chair. Rather they should be in the hands of an experienced behavioural therapist.

"His deeds betray the psychopath", I wrote above. With a little practice you can learn to see through people with a good "hit rate". It's like learning a new language and extremely useful.

State leaders have recognised this as well:

Leading politicians from many countries employ soul researchers to supply them with psychiatric profiles of other rulers. Such information can be rewarding in conversations taken at a "high level", as meanings behind the spoken word become more apparent.

Police profilers do not do anything else. Based on the criminal act and the external circumstances they try, often successfully, to understand the state of mind of the perpetrator. In this way the next criminal act of the person concerned can sometimes be unearthed.

Similarly, trainers of football teams look meticulously at recordings of games, in order to analyse and develop counter-tactics. Psychologists do a similar thing, but use facial expressions, body language and the observance of gestures to come to their conclusions. Among other things, those hosting the next state receptions or diplomatic talks will be better prepared.

In order to expand knowledge or increase power, nothing is left to chance. There is a permanent state mutual observation, which includes phone tapping, spying on emails, control over movement, patterns of behaviour and so on.

The omnipresent control and data gathering mania of authorities and companies, to which we seem to have already become accustomed, shows data protection officers to be toothless tigers and highlights the mental uncertainties of the statesmen and managers. Information advantage offers a certain security. Greed is part of it, but it also compensates for psychological shortcomings as excellent money can be made by it.

"Power makes you sick," one can read in the literature. Those who have power always want more, and **are** already sick. "Power makes you even sicker" fits better. Even those who have **no** power and want to get it, **are** already sick, because a mentally healthy person has no desire to strive for it.

That desire is inhibited by the inner abundance and self-assurance of the healthy person. He or she does not need to subjugate others because they want to be one of them.

A mentally healthy person would never think of provoking or even starting a war.

Mighty people are basically violent people; however, the better ones make use of terror and constraints within "legal" means, and may pass laws to do so. In this way, they legally live out their aggression, whilst the average person acts out their frustrations on the street and get punished for it.

In my experience we have to thank the "lived and ignorant German policy of the last 5 decades" for the increasing German violence by reason of xenophobia or religion. In addition the permanent increase of brutalisation we see in TV programs (to stay competitive) plays a further part.

Over the last 30 years, I have had several thousand conversations with people of all walks of life (**non**-migrant people in this context).

Many Germans are afraid of overpopulation, of alienation, cultural change (ie, minarets in many German cities) and offences resulting from foreign religious beliefs and mentalities.

Incidentally, a popular referendum has been held in Switzerland on whether minarets can be built. The population rejected this in 2009. Since then, there has been a building ban in the Federal Constitution of the Swiss Confederation.

Furthermore, there has been a constant curtailment of freedom of expression partly due to "anti-Semitic" reproaches).

Obviously, the will of the German population is falling on deaf ears among politicians as more and more foreigners have been allowed to enter the country for years. Because of this, German politicians are playing their part in stoking and fanning the flames of further German xenophobia.

In my opinion it is therefore not surprising that at some point aggression breaks out against that particular group of people (thought to be "the enemy") and against those who then have to restore public order. Increasing violence against police officers has been a regular topic in the German media for many years.

The rise of violence in stadiums during football matches is to my mind, simply a welcome opportunity to live out such aggression.

Unfortunately, politicians have never really or sustainably questioned the reasons behind this. Maybe our "people's representatives" do not want to seriously deal with these explosive and uncomfortable social issues, preferring instead to sweep the real reasons under the carpet. It is all too easy to burn your mouth and fingers, and politicians want to continue their career successfully.

If any "result" comes from an updated policy, it is simply to demand tougher punishments, and this does not impress. **Incidentally**, the death penalty in other countries does not prevent murder.

Who needs and wants power? **We are not born with this desire.** What kind of humans are these 🔔 ! and what is their purpose?

Power (and the desire for it) is a clear sign of inner insecurity, mostly based on feelings of powerlessness acquired in earliest youth. See the remarks under "Everyone is the Victim of their Own Education".

Those who have power can reliably hold others down, and ideally do so through the use of other institutions (i.e. the police or the military). In addition, such actions directly help shape draft legislation.

One example is tax law, which is often viewed as disproportionally high and of significantly greater burden to the average worker when compared to the wealthy. This is despite the progression table.

Logically, because the "makers of the laws" (highly-paid) choose not to side against themselves or against "Lobby & Co.". Who saws off the branch on which he sits?

Example: Hence we have the wealth tax and the constant jabbering about its (non-) introduction.

In addition, power can be highly addictive. Older gentlemen beyond the age of 70 in particular, are often happy to be provided with the "responsible position" drug, whilst the normal workers are glad to be able to retire at 60, 63, 65 or 67 years.

A working life usually makes a person so flat that he only wants one thing afterwards: his calm and maybe a few niceties in old age, so long as the pension allows it.

Based on this view, and with our own fathers, grandfathers and great-grandfathers in mind, there exists at least two views:

a) The job as a re-elected senior cannot be so exhausting, especially since dispositions, together with physical and spiritual powers decline rapidly beyond the age of 70.

b) If the said reserves are actually still available, they obviously were not used up in the previous "responsible position". One could then rightly assume that life as a bricklayer or office worker is much more exhausting than a life as a "top" politician.

Presumably then, they did not give as much (unselfish) to "their" people as they always want to make us believe. Yet there's a Federal Cross of Merit or a job as "President of the German Federal Parliament" awaiting a top politician.

A straw man, who is ultimately only used for representation purposes, tends to doze off during speeches and who the people can easily do without, still receives a royal payment from taxpayers.

Another phenomenon:

It is interesting to note that at all times of human domination (and failure), big showmanship and magnificent buildings played a blatant role and still do so. **Palaces are symbols of power** (thick-walls outside and hollow inside, just like most of their users, owners and operators).

Gigantomania (megalomania) was a concise and formative trademark of weak souls of its clients at all times in human history (see also aircraft- and ship-building).

On the one hand, this is to show off ("Look what I have great!", as in the sandbox, see "Infantilism"), and on the other, to intimidate. High, thick walls and magnificent towers are to show others that he has nothing to "decide" here.

However, the walls only have the potential to intimidate those people who have similar mental deficits to the inhabitants themselves. A healthy psyche cannot be impressed by artfully stacked and carved stone blocks.

At the same time the walls protect the accumulated assets and show, of course unintentionally, the high internal vulnerability of the resident or owner.

For example, the construction of the pyramids, which are undoubtedly architectural masterpieces, together with other imposing structures often considered as part of the ancient "Seven Wonders of the World", hardly fulfill any other purpose.

When, until a few centuries ago, the clergy still had great power and influence and were even feared by emperors and kings, the churches and cathedrals often could not be big and the towers not be high enough.

"The largest house is to be dedicated to the **Lord**." That is to be granted to him, but: **He** is mentally perfect, wise and therefore modest, so would undoubtedly be satisfied with a paltry hut.

Cathedral buildings are primarily built not for the Lord, but for those who preach to him. God does not need magnificent buildings and does not need to impress. This is a most human weakness.

See the press reports from the year 2014 regarding the completely exaggerated construction costs of the cathedral in Limburg (Germany). Even a bishop is only human and can succumb to pomp. Vanity and greed are among the Seven Deadly Sins. His suitability for the priestly office should therefore be questioned.

Anyone who has ever studied the pomp of the Vatican, and perhaps even paid a visit to the billions it houses, may wonder: "What's this all about? 🔔! How much hunger and misery in the world could be averted with the equivalent funds? "

Incidentally, "being Pope" is just the supreme rung of a worldly career ladder.

The "Thousand Year Empire" has similar examples such as the “Empire Chancellery” (Reichskanzlei) in Berlin and the "Germania" plans born out of Hitler's megalomania and architectural planning of Albert Speer.

The descendants and modern classics of all splendour and swanky buildings are the “mirror cathedrals” of the banking, car and insurance industries. No bank or insurance company needs iridescent facades and glass domes for their serious business. These will not improve productivity.

The maintenance (or even "only" leasing costs) of the fragile facades costs immense sums, which are finally factored into the account and custody charges of insurance premiums. We all pay for this useless and neurotic delusion.

An appalled observer may ask "how can one regard the buildings of the Vatican, places of worship, buildings of the III. Empire and the houses of business enterprises in the same breath?"

Yes, how one can?! **Answer:** It belongs psychologically together, because when viewed "naked" and without all the circumstantial pomp, they are all control centres of power!

The building example shows that inner worlds are reflected outwardly and affect something there; the architecture and the construction of the outer world. This can be perceived by other people as either emotionally normal or sick.

Walls in the head cause physical walls (eg wall construction of the former German Democratic Republic, planned wall construction USA/Mexico).

Those who are anxious and insecure inside, and feel fragile in the depths, will build thick walls and erect high garden fences (instead of a handsome wooden fence), hold an aggressive dog and install video surveillance systems. It is also possible they may have a firearm to hand in the bedside drawer.

The vernacular says, "If you want to know what happens inside a Human's head, have a look at its storage (or cellar)." Look into the garden and draws of the desk as well.

Another indication for millennia of lived psychic weakness:

In addition to possession and power, titles remove and alienate people from each other. They manifest social differences and represent a form of valorising oneself, of delimiting and distinguishing oneself from "ordinary" people; a kind of balancing contact fears.

Titles want to intimidate and let expect that the "lower degreed" doing more respectful or even submissive. This can still be experienced today, especially in public offices, is firmly in the minds of all and is often applied practice.

Adresses such as academic degrees, director, superior, excellency, eminence, count, duke etc., on balance, say little about the "value" of a person for the entire society or personal merits; possibly something about the level of education.

At best, inherited titles tell you whether someone was born "with a golden spoon in their mouths" without ever having done anything worthwhile; the latter applies primarily to monarchies.

In the structure of a psychic healthy society and togetherness, phrases such as "Mr. Director" or "Your Excellency" are superfluous and ridiculous viewed through a magnifying lense of a mentally healthy person.

Mighty people, whether they work in business or politics, do not deserve our votes. **Rather** they **require our full (medical) attention, our care, our compassion and the care of an experienced psychologist.** Certainly they should never be in positions where they have the opportunity to make momentous decisions.

In fact, elections do nothing, because behind all the statements and decisions is always a sick power-hungry-man with bent soul-lenses and prisms.

The voter and the party in which he or she is a member <u>do not play the slightest role.</u> The party is only a means to an end, which is to get hold of a suitable position.

Just as the form of government or the social system is irrelevant, be it aristocracy, democracy, dictatorship, capitalism or communism, all variations of human governmental constructs flow in one and the same direction.

That direction is to raise the most unqualified people to the top because of their psychological immaturity and mental disfigurement.

Their domination and selfishness can be lived out undisturbed. As a result, a career in this area is only enjoyed by people with defective emotions.

These narcissists are enough to themselves. They only love themselves and, in the highest degree of their malposition, they consider "the rest of the world" as unworthy human beings, mere human-material even.

By the way, a conspiracy theory is currently circulating which suggests the self-proclaimed "upper ten thousand" of this world intend to decimate the number of earthlings by several billion by the end of this century. A few hundred million would be allowed to stay in order to guarantee the elite a feudal system.

It may be philosophised as to whether there is something in this, yet it is not unthinkable given the behaviour of some heads of state or economic moguls.

Even though:
A population reduction is good for the relief of the planet Earth's resources; the race „Human Being" can and may be called an evolutionary dead end:

Despite his intellect (as he calls it), he slowly self-annihilates; without doing anything seriously, consistently and sustainably.

The human mind is more a curse than a blessing; it leads to self-annihilation because it is relatively simple to manipulate and susceptible to the mental illnesses mentioned.

In the end, the human mind **can't** be biophilic (life-affirming), as nature has showed us for billions of years and has continued to develop itself.

Humans will not survive, because the uses and effects of the "mind" tend to be self-centered and not apply to the whole community (including nature).

***The lust for power
is not rooted in strength,
but in weakness.***

(Erich Fromm, German psychoanalyst and social psychologist

The „Cosmic Criminal"

The term "cosmic criminal" was brought into being by me during the development of this work. This thought came to mind as a logical conclusion.

The "criminal" is not meant in the sense of our legal laws.

I don't want to create an explicited definition at all, because

a) the empathic and mentally healthy person may already guess what it is about and

b) the psychopath, in his mental dementia and lack of self-reflection ability, is unable to understand this and will only smile at it as a result, and is once again compulsively looking for ways to circumvent these natural rules.

The depiction of the cosmic criminal should make it clear how dangerous these sick people are for the whole environment and the survival of humanity on a naturally healthy planet Earth.

In suitable positions of power, these people create their own laws, we all have to obey (but not themselves); regardless of whether this is reasonable ... or not.

However, one definition could be, for example, that cosmic crimes include all unethical/immoral acts aimed at exploiting nature and humans for primitive/monetary reasons, no matter how brutal, cruel and contemptuous the ways to achieve the goal.

Everything that brings money and power is allowed, tolerated and   approved. According to this, laws are drawn up, exceptions are made and special permits are issued etc.

But this is not the meaning and goal of nature, which has its own - much stronger laws - which one better obeys.

The cosmic criminal violates these natural laws permanently and vehemently, as if to show that he is stronger than them. We are increasingly feeling the consequences for this and can that can be read and heard in the media almost every day (e.g. global warming and its far-reaching effects).

For example, cosmic crimes are all offenses against nature or rape of them, like

- Cutting down the rain forest,
- all animal experiments without any exception as well,
- Bulk animal husbandry/animal husbandry that is not appropriate to the species and behavior, only for "increases in yield" (shortening beaks and piglet castration without anesthesia, stalls that are too narrow, chickens shredding etc.),
- mass destruction of insects by insecticides and industrial agriculture and over-fertilization of the soil,
- mass tourism including the consequent destruction of habitats worth protecting,
- all wars in human history,
- torture and vivisection,
- disposal of still usable foodstuffs or their restraint in order to be able to achieve higher prices later; or even the destruction of intact goods,
- use of the oceans as waste disposal,

- separation of children from their parents,
- separations of countries via construction of walls,
- arms trade,
- Trials and use of all kinds of nuclear weapons.

These examples are a small selection and could certainly be continued over several pages.
In principle, all violence against animals can be viewed as representative of violence against people or their community. The perpetrator/animal torturer has found a way to (partly socially accepted and legally sanctioned) channeling his aggressions, which he can live out almost without punishment (incl. "Livestock" animal husbandry).

If people inflicted these acts on people, it would result in severe punishments.

The Solution

Democracy is the smallest evil within the framework of the known forms of government, and exists so we may live and get along largely without serious conflicts of interest. However, it has one drawback in that all have to yield to the majority. If all accept this, nothing should stand in the way of peaceful coexistence.

It is completely without doubt, democracy is a fine thing, if it works. **Unfortunately it does not work,** at least not the way the base model envisaged. Life in general for the average citizen is a sham package, with democratic rights being minimised as far as possible.

Ever since the invention of structures and laws, people have tried to undermine, soften, annul, abuse and interpret them to suit their own interest. The higher you stand in the hierarchy, the greater your chances of this type of success. That is why, in my view, **democracy as it is currently practised, is the weakest form of dictatorship.**

Democracy, as it is now commonplace in many countries, is the feudalism of postmodernity as we know it today.

When the French liberated themselves via revolution from the aristocracy and their feudal rule with the lavish and arrogant debauchery, they certainly wanted to regain control over themselves.

The memory of the guillotine has clearly defused in the course of the last 230 years. Now, chancellors, state presidents and the like can again let themselves go unpunished, patronise the people and live parasitically and decadently at their expense. The source of this money can be forgotten.

Every few years there is a hewing and stinging around the popular (read: highly doped) government posts. These posts offer the highest levels of soapiness, power, "being heard", luxury living, free travel and sometimes small black suitcases with a few surprises to boot!

How else could one explain intelligently that a few years, well let's be kind and call it "work" as a deputy, is more important than the lifetime performance of a diligent worker? Better said the worker is mocked.

Is there a reasonable case for that? The answer is very clear: **No!** But there is at least one **un**reasonable argument, which is that whoever can grant themselves a generous salary plus more rights, will do so if they are emotionally deformed enough. This can be termed the "pay and perks-self-service store".

The opinion of the elected person comes to the fore, and no longer folk's will: **the sick psyche of the elected person is the weak point of democracy.**

In our economy, those with the broadest salaries, bonus payments and the like are the most brazen. It is striking that the highest salaries often go to those who do the most damage.

If paid exclusively on performance, each apprentice of the same company would have to receive a higher renumeration than the boss.

The best paid one could argue, is someone who takes occupational responsibility. In our society this is always much better paid than manual work. We can talk about that.

However, which "top" politician or economic mogul has ever actually taken responsibility or faced the consequences of driving the cart into the wall?

Often a resignation is offered or demanded, yet some cling to their position because:

a) it would mean a loss of power (very bad for a power neurotic) and

b) it could be a certain admission that they might have done something wrong (self-reflection topic). It could also threaten a "loss of face".

The self-chosen and "noble" resignation of such a person means a crash into a well-padded warm nest. In fact, we do not need to worry about whether he or she is well cared for, as the pension entitlements are maintained at a high level.

The "hewing and stinging" already mentioned above is commonly called an "election campaign". From all sides and parties the "people's representatives" (because they are likely to be displaced) suddenly crawl out of their holes and get themselves as close to the people as they can.

They try with a good deal of Pseudo altruism* and verbal diarrhea, to pull people onto their side, so they can exercise their neuroses as far as possible for another legislative period; legally of course!

(* **Pseudo altruism:** Altruism means colloquially, to show respect, disinterestedness and selflessness to his fellow human beings. Socially, this may translate as "charity." Pseudo-altruism, therefore, signifies that these things are merely played out, a deception to accomplish things that are otherwise difficult to accomplish.)

It would be nice if our politicians would campaign for the citizen as vehemently as they scramble for posts after the new elections.

These people disrespectfully throw insults to each other in full view of the television cameras. A reasonably educated citizen would not address their children in such a way.

The opposing candidates spread lies, blame and election promises which, as we all regularly experience, are barely upheld.

Even so one cannot blame them, because their first experiences, impressions or serious communication outside of the family take place when they are pupils in elementary or lower secondary school.

Here rules the principle of the "biggest mouth", although in this period of life it is still "allowed" and can be termed infantilism*. Whoever clicks their fingers loudest can best interrupt, because even the toughest teacher at some point will become annoyed by constant clicking or interjection.

Almost always we have (in my experience) the finger-clicking "in-between-talker", who then jabbers the most nonsense.

However, they succeed in distributing their verbal trash among the people. This important experience is taken into adult behaviour because it has brought personal benefits.

*Infantilism: (= Latin infantilis = childish) means in psychol. Context "stopped at the level of childhood". The body has continued to grow, but the behaviour no longer corresponds to age. One can speak of an emotional immaturity, which manifests itself in undisciplined behaviour, i.e. repeated interjections, lack of self-reflection, defiance, self-centeredness, disrespect or provocative behaviour. Illustratively speaking, a jacket that has been fitted in childhood, has never been taken off and is still worn despite the tensed stitching and strained material.

The really knowing pupils tend to wait discreetly and work out what is going on. An experienced pedagogue knows that.

Who wants to complain seriously about politics, annoyance and electoral fatigue when so much nonsense is discussed?

In addition, these ladies and gentlemen want to explain to us what is "politically correct": One worries about whether and why one should not for example use the term "Negro" for dark-skinned people, rather than the currently called "Maximum Pigmented". The half-life of such term-changes are shortening rapidly.

As a result, albinos (people with albinism) should now be labeled "minimal pigmented" in order to be politically correct and respectful.

It is a thought-prison, whose warden, guard and moral apostle we place every few years via election in the saddle of the high horse.

....and so the citizen sees himself at the mercy of dubious figures, which he chose for lack of a reasonable alternative.

When the time comes for us to make important choices again, let's think things through.

If one compares this behaviour, especially the "TV-talking-duels" held during these election-lies, to the childhood of those concerned, one sees nothing other than children in the sandpit throwing dirt at each other. For days on end the media have nothing better to do than "analyse" the infantile fuss. How seriously can we take it?!

In general, one could say: "Those who want to rule should first learn to master themselves."

On the evening of the election, everything is picked up to the smallest detail by the press, what if, ..., and if not, what would happen then? And: Who now with whom and why not ....? Mental masturbation in high potency!

If the result is positive there is general back-slapping and self praise, but if the result is negative there follows a stunned "what have we done wrong?!" This means that even when blatantly wrong decisions are made, there is no consideration of the consequences, no self-reflection and no thought of what could arise from it. Self-glorifying and narcissism are always to the fore.

Now I would like to throw a few tomatoes, because the examples are so vividly illustrative and have been shown around the world in the media. The examples that follow show such steep templates they almost scream for acceptance and review:

An act of self-expression, an act of narcissism:
The selection of the venue for the G20 summit on the 7th and 8th of July 2017 was Hamburg.

This is the **birthplace** of Mrs. Merkel, and as mentioned in the press, she wanted to bring the visitors closer to her.

The result was heavy riots. These supposedly were not foreseeable in the immediate vicinity of Hamburg's "Schanzenviertel" district, an area known to be problematic in relation to politics.

One might think that the state security, which investigates any arson on a Syrian stroller, probably slept deeply or did not do its homework.

What even Klein Erna (the famous little-girl-mascot of Hamburg) from "Jungfernstieg" would know, seemed not to be clear to the public agency, or so it appeared.

Let's carry on.....:

Extensive disturbances to the daily business of inhabitants and traders, as well as to public transport ensued. Residents could not go out due to massive police barriers and had to stay in their flats and homes. Parents could not pick up their children from daycare and there was high property damage.

We were told and had to read **"It had to be a densely urban area!"** The background was that the population or participants of the G20 summit can get in touch with each other.

However, this was due to the hermetic security precautions which were an illusion from the outset.

Another illustrative example:

Mrs. Merkel's Welcome Policy for Refugees during September 2015, was to let some hundreds of thousands enter Germany without any registration.

In terms of ignorance and impertinence this single handed act is hard to surpass. It clearly says: "I'll do what I want anyway" (Defiance), and "we will continue to do it." It seems to many Germans this is an **anti-native policy**.

The Nobel Peace Prize was awarded exactly during that period of time. (🔔   Ring, ring, ring...)

The press, politicians and various experts from abroad all agreed this did much to promote further terrorism in Europe, and provide an improved, broad basis to prepare and covertly implement further assassinations.

Finally and lastly:

Following the general election on 24.09.2017, some almost never-ending negotiations, meetings and exploratory talks concerning the formation of a new government followed.

It took almost six full months to set up and present a new government to (hopefully) fulfill the electoral mandate. The lucrative Ministerial posts were awarded within a few days. If only the finding of common interests were as fast!

How is it that experienced and hopefully mature people (often seniors) were not able to "come together" and develop a meaningful plan? Do party programs diverge so much?!

Any capable boss in the private sector would have dissolved this working group after two or three weeks and replaced them with new, more competent and willing people.

What is it all about? It is about leading a people responsibly and successfully through the next legislative period. How different are the goals of the individual parties that one cannot find a common denominator and get together?

It's all about one thing after all, and that's why you cannot find each other 🔔 !:

Power claim, calculatio, not giving away one centimeter, loss of face and as far as possible to avoid, refusing to accept anyone else may be correct!

Disease of the soul prevents cooperation and costs millions every year.

Mental disorders are big rocks in the gear of politics and economics. Without these "rocks," every human being on earth would be able to live in peace, have good food and drink and share a clean environment with all nature's creatures.

Politicians and rulers are an obsolete model and as soon as possible should be abolished. There is a much better solution way.

Politicians
are spirits of third class.

Mahatma Gandhi

(Indian freedom fighter)

My first urgent demand:

Have psychology taught in all Federal schools several times per week as a main subject along side English, German and Mathematics from the fourth elementary grade!

The main reason is so children and adolescents have the opportunity to see through the subtle and perfidious methods of the advertising industry, which via the mass stultification weapons of TV and Internet, often draw scarce funds from their pockets.

The psycho terror in the supermarkets with its psychologically determined sales tricks is another reason. Here, psychology is abused to massively manipulate people for the primitive purpose of expanding sales and maximising profits, which usually flow into very few pockets.

Studies have shown that well over 90% of all information that reaches our brains every day is aimed at our wallet.

Advertising is attempted manipulation and thus attempted fraud, and the same applies to the election campaigns.

Unfortunately, this attempted fraud is procedurally intangible and hence not punishable.

My second insistent demand (as an intermediate step):

Psychological proficiency tests for business leaders and politicians from the immediate leadership cadre, and annual compulsory training by experienced psychologists and professionals on how to deal responsibly with people and the environment.

But better, Thirdly (the second is still necessary for economic leaders):

The Referendum Republic:

So-called "e-voting" (electronic voting) is a forward-looking system, although perhaps not yet fully mature, as shown by the difficulties in US elections especially concerning the reliable counting of votes. These teething problems however, could be eliminated in the medium term if it were seriously wanted.

By the way, this system is of course applicable for each nation in the world. The German reference is only an example.

Although fraud can never be ruled out, we have after all been paying with credit cards and buying goods online for decades with virtually no technical problems. Wherever money flows or should flow, it is usual for everything to go both fast and smooth, in both planning and execution.

In Germany, the "leadership elite" continues to hide behind the Constitution (Basic Law), and e-voting is "at least constitutionally, not a viable option." Why not change the constitution?

What a crude thought! It would also be inconvenient, because of work responsibilities, and give all of the German electorate more rights to represent themselves, use their own brains and limit some rights of politicians.

Unfortunately, we do not find creative and courageous minds among (German) politicians. The "I do not dare...." virus is widespread and sits deep. Fear makes people stiff and inflexible and paralyses the body and mind. Their souls have been stiff for decades.

Then you have to have the courage to work on the Basic Law. After all, like everything else in life, this naturally has more than just a few wrinkles after about 70 years and is in dire need of refurbishment so it will not be too tight for the young and aspiring people of this country. In fact, no major change in the constitution is needed:

There is only a change required in the legislative area. These days the so-called "legislative power", the German Federal Parliament (Bundestag) and Federal Council of Germany (Bundesrat) are being replaced directly by the German nation. The federal and state parliaments as well as some committees are no longer necessary, and the people of Germany can finally represent themselves.

One problem lies in the composition of the 709 members of the Bundestag who represent us, which by no means reflects the electorate (as of the 19th Bundestag at the end of September 2017). There can be no talk of representation. It is more of an "overintellectualisation" that does not include reality at the workbench and on the street, or that cannot be included due to lack of experience.

It is not unusual for a degree program to end with the candidate going directly to the "green table" (a German saying which means making major decisions without any life experience) without ever getting to know the hard working life.

The result is the following picture (quotes; bundestag.de, Wikipedia, daily press):

a) In 115 lawyers, the total share of academics is over 90 percent.

b) About 20% of the members are over 60 years old and in individual cases aged up to 77 years (with more than 50% aged between 45 and 59 years).

c) The quota of women in the Bundestag is far below that demanded by the government. There are only 211 women in a parliament of 491 men.

Back to e-voting:

The entertainment industry has been successfully using e-voting on a small scale for many years. We know it under the name "Ask-the-Audience-lifeline" in a popular knowledge game for the famous million. This is a vivid example of electronically applying and implementing democracy and knowledge.

This system not only uses the knowledge of all people in the audience (collective intelligence), but takes one very big and rewarding step further. Of course, not everyone involved in the selection is 100 percent sure of the correct answer, but the "gut feeling" in the decision adds a significant amount of emotional intelligence.

The logical mind is an important tool for making decisions in life, yet how many times have we been right when the gut (the heart) felt otherwise? We do not have to be able to justify everything with words because sometimes the spirit is right.

The Referendum Republic makes intensive use of collective and emotional intelligence and, like no other system, represents the will of the citizens, directly and therefore feels close to the people. A more pure democracy model is not thinkable or representable.

The rest is pure technology and basically already implemented, if you look at the daily practice of online petitions of various concerns, which is also - and especially - applied internationally.

Another example can be seen in online banking, credit card shopping, the ordering of goods online and in other aspects of everyday life we use personal identification numbers. This is normal practice in everyday life.

Yet, with today's implementation of democracy, we still live as we did 150 years ago.

Now every citizen with voting rights gets his "voting account". This could be operated via the Social Security number and would be unique to everyone. This voting account is maintained and guided at home via the citizen's PC.

Anyone who does not have or want a PC can vote in an election office (as before). Election dates or periods are announced via the voting account and via radio, television and newspapers. These appointments can run for several days or even weeks, giving everyone the time and opportunity to vote. One is therefore not limited to just one election day.

The respective voting topic is presented with the most important pros and cons, so that every voter has the possibility to get detailed information.

However, this is not to elect political parties or members of parliament, but is to decide direct action on proposals of greater significance.

Less urgent topics can be summarised and regularly scheduled, perhaps for intervals of around 3 months.

Proposals as to what should be decided may be submitted by each voter to a nationwide central office, as a sub-item in the voting account. This would be divided into subject areas with respective sub-points, similar to the telephone selection procedures in the complaints departments of large companies.

If many similar or identical proposals come together over time, this can be brought to a vote via the voting account.

Of course, this system could not manage without administration, but then there would be enough empty buildings and offices previously used by politicians and their entourages.

The fact money is always and increasingly of utmost importance, degenerates into the main argument:

The new system would save billions of taxpayers' money. Expenses such as diets, pensions, building maintenance (i.e. the Reichstag building and country parliaments), personal security and armoured luxury cars are only a small selection of what could be saved.

Saved money could then be used more meaningfully, ie for modernisation, construction and extension of educational institutions, kindergartens and such.

In addition to the enormous savings mentioned above, there are other noteworthy advantages which follow:

- The elimination of sleaze, personal sensivities and the effects of neurotic disorders among the government "power people", together with a sustainable abolition of personal benefits. Let's stop leading them into temptation.

- In future, no lobbying or the distortion of decisions caused by competitive conditions.

- The elimination of party donations with their partly shady character. (By the way, the donation suitcases have to got bigger with the planned abolishment of the 500 Euro banknote.)

- The statement "all state power comes from the people" would finally get a real and credible meaning. This is political self-control and direct self-determination on the part of the citizen. Democracy in pure culture!

In any case the whole thing deserves economic consideration in relation to cost-benefits:

While companies around the world are cutting costs drastically, saving staff and outsourcing, every country in the world has a well-cushioned government. Germany, for example, maintains the second largest parliament in the world (after the giant country of China).

The German governmental apparatus (709 parliamentarians) costs taxpayers several hundred million euros per year. We can have a much less expensive government with a significantly higher output.

Even more grotesque is that millions of citizens of some countries subsidise the pomp of a monarchy:

Millions work hard day by day to allow a very few members of the "amusement elite" to live in the lap of luxury, and do gymnastics through the beds to produce the next vain heir to the throne (to be applauded and venerated as if they had won the Nobel Prize).

The royally paid work in politics cannot be so time-consuming and exhausting, because many deputies are also engaged in demanding and lucrative occupations such as for example, the operation of a law firm.

Years ago in the "Berliner Adendschau" (the Berlin Evening Show), a young member of the Berlin Senate said he did not understand how many of his colleagues could perform such demanding tasks on the side, because the work of a member of parliament was a full time job if exercised responsibly. A statement that makes you look deeply.

With the rapid progress in all areas of technology, it is actually a wonder that the political system continues and remains the same. Maintaining power at any price is certainly desired.

The components of human political failure can be eliminated in this way to 99.9%, taking into account that no electoral fraud takes place.

Politicians as "leaders" and decision makers are superfluous in the "Referendum Republic".

A permanently trained and mentally sound diplomatic corps is sufficient to maintain a lively and friendly contact with the co-countries and to perform domestic representation tasks.

These Corps get the political orders directly from the competent Federal Office, which has counted the votes on the election proposals, and ensure that people's democratic opinions will be represented at all levels.

The voter does not go to the polls every 4 or 5 years, but designs and lives his democracy constantly. There are no more legislative periods. The results are implemented immediately and the citizen sees in the short term, what has become of it.

Electoral fatigue will disappear when the citizen realises that his or her efforts really are of benefit and taken seriously.

There is no doubt that there is much to think through in terms of practical implementation. However, "where there is a will, there is also a way, "and "where there is no will, no way shall be found."

In the Free Economy.....

..... things do not look any better in view of leadership behaviour and the dirt it stirs up.

Also industry rages on "faster, higher, further", because as in government, mentally disfigured business bosses want to be admired and their feelings of inferiority exercised daily.

Take for example, the car companies affair with their "Lobby Thick" and criminal excesses in terms of global emission. In this instance they lied and cheated, just to get better numbers (not actual values). It's just "too bad" that at some point everything comes into the light of day ...... and that's a good thing!

How naive that many believed this scam would remain secret forever. This is not only terrifying and embarrassing, but extremely stupid. It indicates that such people do not have the psychological qualification to lead corporations.

Just a few decades ago, only a few people in "high" managerial positions energetically and criminally cheated their companies. Today however, entire boards collectively deceive the companies they preside over.

The further "above" one looks around in the hierarchy of big business, the more detached are the views, which is something reflected in the daily routines. They live their own life, no matter what others think, and escape the realities in a Teflon-coated suit.

Generally, executives worldwide still do not understand that their employees are the most valuable assets to their business. Although this is repeatedly stated as "lip service", it is not implemented or truly believed.

A widespread misbelief of employers is that because they pay a wage or salary, they also own the employees dignity, free time and yes, his whole life.

Only contented employees "produce" satisfied customers, and satisfied customers usually become regular customers.

Entrepreneurs renounce about 30% of their revenue annually worldwide. This is only an average and in individual cases it could be "only" 20% or as much as 50%. Lack of leadership qualities (i.e. so-called "Bossing", which means bullying directed by the boss to the employee) is the main reason, although in addition the wrong selection of personnel and bad product management play a part.

Companies, which have a liberal and responsive management structure, can be pleased about the above-mentioned additional income (including savings by, for example, avoiding the training of new employees due to high fluctuation - better "flight"uation).

Back to the employees:

An employee who is dissatisfied will not as a rule, resign immediately. The principle of inertia applies both in physics and on a personal level. Only when a certain degree of intensity has been reached, when time has run out and when the suffering becomes unbearable, is action is taken.

In the interim however, the employee quits from in the inside and stops working honestly for the firm. They may even do sabotage or steal, something not often noticed immediately by the management. His colleagues, who may also feel the same, can be "infected", take part and say nothing to the boss.

This can cause great damage, but management has to take some responsibility as it is their attitude that causes the employees to behave in such a way.

By the way, it is usual for a healthy working group to deal with an individual "lazybones" via group dynamics. A boss is not usually needed and has no need to worry. In extreme cases however, the boss can still intervene.

"Do you have references?" We mostly know this phrase from television. Anyone who applies for a new area of activity should be able to prove that he or she is capable of doing a good job.

It seems to me the "higher" the status of the applicant, the less is asked by way of qualifications. This is most **unfortunate**.

Old cliques from study days are often used, or someone owes someone else a favour to fall up some stairs. It is little wonder therefore that incompetents who have been marauding in XY's executive board and then driven out with some million Pound payoff without loss of face, now sit on the supervisory board of company YZ.

Vitamin "B" requires no knowledge and skills. All it needs is a portion of mental disorder and an influential circle of friends and acquaintances that place no value on sustainable integrity.

It is no wonder derailments of many kinds follow, because nothing has been learnt from previous calamities (lack of self-reflection).

If we are already on the subject of staff, a word to the staff of the Human Resources Departments:

In the last two to three decades, the focus is only on who wrote the most flawless application or CV. For the most part, the person behind the application has become completely uninteresting.

Even the most brilliant candidate, ideal for the corporation, fails because some small, completely minor spelling mistakes exclude him or her from the outset. Even a secretary can (and may!) make a typo.

What 'smart' heads have come up with this and act out their control neuroses?!

Saying someone is "overqualified" is hard to beat for stupidity. It is and should be up to each person to decide for which job they want to apply and work at in future.

The only important thing is that the new employee is an asset to the company. After all, how small-minded and shabby it is to judge a person solely on spelling mistakes, or whether the photo sticks too far to the left in the upper right-hand side of the page!

What works in politics, business and work is frequently found in the family:

The after-work tyrant. This person vents their day time frustrations caught from the boss, employees, traffic and other people on the bus and train on their family.

Thus the weaker members of society, including the children, are subjected to some of the neuroses of those who educate them.

In this way, the cycle continues and as adults these children go on to terrorise their children in a similar way.

> *..., but if you want to test*
> *a man's character,*
> *give him power.*
> Abraham Lincoln

Afterword

"What luck for the governors

that Humans do not think!"

From whom may these words come? The author is Adolf Hitler from January 1942/Wolfsschanze.

"My God," the reader may now think, "Now he's coming with this...!"

That is completely understandable. After all, German media, and in particular German television, never tires of showing the life of this gentleman almost every evening, illuminated from all sides. Hitler was a bad person who still makes us a lot of money today. Where is the moral? It has been on holiday for decades!

The guilty conscience of Germans in the Xth post-war generation is kept alive and generates a lot of money.

"Those who have not mastered their past cannot deal with their futures in a sustainable way. I learned this years ago from my studies of psychology. This is certainly true not only for each individual, but also for an entire nation.

Obviously, we still have not mastered the German past. If we had Germany could at last look after its own future in a sustainable manner and divert millions of Euros (used today for compensation payments) toward the future of our children (i.e. the urgent updating of schools, universities and the like).

No one still holds a grudge against France for the Napoleonic wars, but does this mean Germany must wait another 100 years for absolution?

Yet there is another much more recent shame. Decades after WW2, the Germany of 2017 is the third largest arms exporter worldwide (after the USA and Russia).

If someone had predicted this in the 1950s they would not have been believed, and most likely would have been laughed at.

While radical right-wing extremists are being fought in Germany to stave off a possible revival of a III. German Empire and maintain peace, German politicians produce weapons and export them to crisis areas.

In Germany the gun laws are tightened ever further, yet the responsible parliamentarians are apparently content for their arms exports to inflict death, mutilation and devastation upon millions of people, animals and the environment. Unquestionably these persons are accomplices to atrocities.

Probably none of our political acrobats have ever considered that the same weapons can also be used in a roundabout way against German soldiers or the civilian population.

The interdependencies and commitments with the various alliances are not a credible argument in favor of this, but rather serve as a hypocritical justification for making extremely lucrative arms export deals.

The German Basic Law Art. 26 (1) and (2) is trampled with feet here, and since then the victims of the Second World War have been constantly derided by German arms exports.

Arms' trading is an expression of a blatant personal inner weakness shared by all politicians and deputies, who support, vote or otherwise approve. This applies to all nationalities, cultures and religions who take part in this type of trade.

For that reasons, there will never be a world peace, because with war can be earned a lot of money and also gives soul-sick state leaders and their vassals the opportunity to live out their inferiority feelings.

A revealing field of activity of the psychopath is **destructiveness** in all directions; in this sense, a destructive attitude and the actions that lead to it.

To say **"no"** to arms' trading is to show strength.

We can subvert the double moral standard with another example as follows. For decades, our "power elite" have struggled with hands and feet to prevent the legalising of Cannabis. The main argument is that this entry-level drug can easily lead to the future use of harder drugs such as heroin, cocaine and the like.

The real reason however is fear of declining sales in the pharmaceutical industry. When used responsibly, as Cannabis

151

usually is, there are almost no side effects and it is very low cost. This contrasts greatly to the many expensive drugs (i.e. analgesics) promoted by the pharmaceutical industry, who fear loss of demand.

Alcohol and cigarettes are allowed. After all, many millions of taxpayers' money is flushed into the public purse each year, yet the undeniable health risks and consequences play only a subordinate role. Those of a nervous disposition should not study the health and social consequences of smoking and alcoholism in any detail.

For example, the "deterrent" images on the cigarette packs are, figuratively speaking, no more than a "cartoon".

Studies in this area have revealed that it is primarily spirits that open the way to the harsher drug world, and not Cannabis.

Should this prompt a responsible decision maker to ban alcohol and nicotine in their entirety (see the Prohibition period in the US from 1920 to 1933)? That would be true stupidity, because these substances keep the masses quiet: "Opium for the people" (Karl Marx referred to religion with these words).

Politicians are mentally inflexible in their roles, are usually resistant to conclusive arguments (unreasonable) and have a "I do not dare ....." mind set. Those who stick meticulously to the status quo are not suitable for such offices.

It is interesting to observe that young people in politically responsible positions, who should know the problems of their generational comrades and be mentally flexible, are often subject to a spontaneous early senescence.

How else could it be explained that many innovative and sparkling ideas soon disappear in the mental aberration of the ruling caste? Anyone who wants to implement their own ideas, who sometimes dares to go it alone and is brave enough to actually say a few clear words, is uncomfortable and does not make progress with their career. Yes-persons desired rather than decision makers.

This was a small digression into the inconsistencies and double standards of the German health system and tax policy.

Back to the actual chapter:

Mr. Hitler has a lot to do with the topic of this book. He is a frightening example of what is possible with a deformed soul, stemming in part from the impact of his childhood and especially the relationship with his father.

But more importantly: Was Adolf Hitler really correct in his personal awareness, as expressed in his words above?

(See also: Erich Fromm: Anatomy of Human Destructiveness, Chapter 13: Malignant Aggression: Adolf Hitler, A Clinical Case of Necrophilia page 415 uff.).

Do people <u>really</u> not think, and is that a blessing to the governors?

Or is it simply more or less indifferent to us what a few psychopaths around the world, who see themselves as infallible "leadership elite" (as also shown via body language, despite image advice and training), decide above our heads what happens to us, what we must think, read, write, do or be allowed to have?

Hence the game is repeated at (ire-)regular intervals with all the likes of Hitler, Stalin, Pol Pot, Mussolini and others, in all shades and facets of psychological weaknesses. All of them can be thought of as humanly failed existences.

Mental cripples unfortunately do not die out but regrow. Just as those regrow again and again, so do so-called followers and freeloaders who prosper from these psychological sick people, through promises of favour. So it happens that history teaches us that it does not teach us anything!

But this is also a constant!

It is interesting that currently only around 250 people (plus tens of thousands of entourage, lobbyists and vicarious agents) rule over the well-being and woes of almost eight billion others (status 2017).

That this will finally change and around 8 billion people will decide over around 8 billion people is high time.

I would like to finish by passing on a remarkable experience. When I was travelling in Namibia in 1998 and was visiting various lodges, I read an article in a German-language magazine that was on display.

The "Deutsch-Südwester", as the descendants of the former colonialists in the former "German Southwest Africa" are still called today, maintain a solid tradition and cohesion as well as the German language.

The magazine "The Insider" was banned in the Federal Republic of Germany. There you could see from an article that the respective (future) German Chancellor had to be "sanctioned" regarding integrity and loyalty whilst taking office by the US government.

What appeared to be conceivable and reasonably acceptable shortly after the Second World War, during 50 years of rebuilding and during the Cold War (1998), became inconceivable about nine years after the fall of the 1989 fall of the Berlin Wall. The reunification in 1990 and contradicted all democratic practices.

Did this corresponded to reality or even still correspond? Well, everyone is allowed to philosophise about this and decide for themselves. Why should the author have been lying? In addition, the vernacular says every "fairy tale has a true core"!

In any case, it is imaginable and not entirely unthinkable or absurd.

Finally and in summary I conclude as follows:

Neuroses are fundamentally necrophilic in nature and not only affect the wearer, but also as a rule, the environment and nature.

Common sense can only come from a healthy soul that feels connected to the community of all.

Psychopaths as described in this book are sick people who cannot serve reliably.

Healthy, or rather "biophilic" decisions cannot be made by these people. Neurotics are unable to do so because they have no objective view on things. It leads to constant failure and to the detriment of all humanity, the environment and nature.

This has been so ever since there have been "chiefs", tribal princes, kings, leaders, prime ministers, chancellors and presidents who want to rule and, worse still, wage and foment wars in the expectation that we believe it is necessary and inevitable.

Nothing and no one should have to serve another and even be proud of it. This is especially so in an army or similar military-organised construct, such as a corporation.

It is not surprising that the normal human being as a (relatively) psychologically healthy man or woman often does not grasp these crude, absurd and egoistic decisions.

Yes, it cannot be understand in any case. It lacks the disease as a prerequisite and psychological coding to follow this and to understand.

As long as we allow psychopaths to sit in our governments and business enterprises, we need expect nothing else but the ruthless exploitation and destruction of the earth and its population.

Neurotics cannot convincingly implement and represent the interests of entire nations that live in peace with each other and tolerantly exchange views.

Expecting this from a powerful man would be as unbelievable as if a five-year child were to be telling jokes about the marriage of his parents.

The history of mankind would have been significantly different over the millennia if the psyche of the responsible ruler or politician had been sound. There would be more peace and much more satisfaction without politicians and emotionally deformed business leaders. We would also have much less environmental destruction.

All of the psychologically handicapped and empathic dead within politics and economics described in this book are not entirely useless, **as they serve to show a functioning society the definition of a "bad example!"**

We should be very vigilant, remain and never stop thinking, questioning and watching so that we finally move on to a contemporary and democratically developed system of governance that works not only at its core, but also in daily life!

We should never stop

doubting "authorities"!

Book Recommendations:

Further and in addition, the following books are recommended:
(written in German)

Psychologie für Jedermann
Pierre Daco
mvg-Verlag
ISBN: 9783636071576

Lassen Sie der Seele Flügel wachsen
Peter Lauster
Rowohlt-Verlag
ISBN: 9783499173615

Lassen Sie sich nichts gefallen
Peter Lauster
Rowohlt-Verlag
ISBN: 9783499620386

Die Neurosen der Chefs
Hesse/Schrader
Eichborn-Verlag,
ISBN-13: 9783821838236

Nieten in Nadelstreifen
Günter Ogger
Knaur-Verlag
ISBN: 9783426771365

www.ingramcontent.com/pod-product-compliance
Lightning Source LLC
Chambersburg PA
CBHW051058250726
48656CB00001B/358